Praise for *The Same but Different*

"A thoughtful, well-written, inside view of the world of twins from a psychologist who is herself a twin—what better vantage from which to shed light on the 'mystique' of twins?"

—*Ricardo Ainslie, PhD, Professor, Educational Psychology, University of Texas at Austin, and author of* The Psychology of Twinship

"Not only is *The Same but Different* a must-read for adult twins, it is an invaluable resource for the parents of younger twins who want to start their same-age childr[...] [...]other of twins

"Dr. F[...]man fully ac[...] twins. Twins, howe[...], need to extr[...] [...]ed fixed roles in ord[...] to live full and [...] a bond no longe[...] [...]ned by all [...] [...]this book[...] adult t[...] and to all [...]

[...] University [...] [...] and author [...] Fetus to Child [...]ins in the World

"As a[...] only child myself and now the mother of twin boys, I greatly appreciate Joan's candid lens into the unique dynamics of the twin relationship. I value the perspective and strategies on raising twins as individuals to develop a self beyond their twin."

—*Amanda Marijanovic, Associate Director, Stella & Dot, personal stylist, and mother of twins*

"This book is a must-read for parents of twins. Joan Friedman highlights some of the complicated challenges facing adult twins and offers guidance for promoting healthy, respectful relationships."

—*Eve Currin, mother of college-age twins*

"Finally, an honest discussion about the realities of being a twin. This book sheds hugely important light on the unique complications that are part of all twins' lives.... Essential reading for twins, spouses of twins, parents and families of twins, and anyone who wants to know what being a twin is really like."

—*Neil Lowenthal, identical twin*

"I know that as my school-age twins approach adolescence and adulthood, I will return many times to the helpful insights and strategies Dr. Friedman offers in *The Same but Different*. This is a book all parents of twins should read—and share with their children when the time is right."

—*Jane Roper, author of* Double Time: How I Survived—and Mostly Thrived—through the First Three Years of Mothering Twins

"*The Same but Different* is for any twin who has ever wondered, 'Why can't others understand me?' or 'Why can't my friendships and romantic relationships be as close as my relationship with my twin?' The book also offers invaluable help and support on issues ranging from how to cope with the endless comparisons to codependency and how to establish healthy relationships outside of one's twinship."

—*Patricia East, PhD, Developmental Psychologist, Department of Pediatrics, Division of Child Development and Community Health, University of California, San Diego School of Medicine*

"This book clearly outlines ways in which twins may struggle as they strive for individuality while trying to maintain their bond....Dr. Friedman allows parents of twins to understand and support their children while giving teen and adult twins deep insight into their own behavior patterns."

—*Gina Osher, "The Twin Coach"*

"This is the book I've been searching for through most of my adult life. I now feel far less alone and more understood in dealing with my lifelong twin-related struggles. Dr. Friedman has provided a road map that previously didn't exist for the confusing, frustrating, and exhilarating experience of being a twin."

—*Mark Lowenthal, identical twin*

"Joan Friedman is one of those rare twins experts who tells the whole truth about the experience of being born alongside another person, growing up constantly lumped and compared. *The Same but Different* explores the powerful complexities of trying to build separate friendships, careers, and romances when one is paired—genetically and societally—with another person. Required reading for adult twins and the people closest to them."

—*Abigail Pogrebin, author of* One and the Same: My Life as an Identical Twin *and* What I've Learned about Everybody's Struggle to Be Singular

"Explores how twinship impacts individuals who are twins and the ways that twins learn to relate to other people in their lives. This book asks twins to consider their personhood both within and without their twinship and to embark on a journey that will foster the development of healthy and satisfying relationships with cotwins, friends, and significant others."
                    —*Caroline Tancredy, PhD, Professor of Psychology, University of Illinois at Urbana-Champaign*

"A well-written, well-organized, and extremely insightful book about the psychological development of twins and the kinds of issues they face throughout adulthood.... The book was not only personally very reassuring but as a professional it was enlightening as well."
                    —*Carolyn S. Spiro, MD, coauthor of* Divided Minds: Twin Sisters and Their Journey through Schizophrenia

"This book will make us better parents, better siblings, better friends, and for twins, better selves."
                    —*Alex Cohen, mother of eighteen-year old identical twins*

"*The Same but Different* is a masterfully written tribute to the complexity of the twin relationship. Reading this book, rich in case studies and insights, is like sitting in on a brilliant psychotherapy session. Joan Friedman takes on the burdensome myth that twins have harmonious relationships and in so doing frees twins to work through their true ambivalence about this key relationship. Her work is also essential reading for all of us mental health professionals who tend to either marginalize or mythologize the twin relationship."
                    —*Frederick K. Miller, MD, PhD, Chair, Department of Psychiatry and Behavioral Sciences, Board of Directors Endowed Chair of Academic Medicine, NorthShore University HealthSystem, and Clinical Associate Professor, University of Chicago Pritzker School of Medicine*

"This book offers a deep and thoughtful exploration of the experience of being a twin and the route toward individual development through the minefield of opposing desires regarding sameness and difference. It recognizes that each twinship is as unique as the individual twins in it."
                    —*Vivienne Lewin, psychoanalytic psychotherapist, London, author of* The Twin in the Transference, *and contributor to* Siblings in Development

"Dr. Joan Friedman's book *The Same but Different* gives important insights into the challenging process of how to separate and individuate from one's twin. Through adult twin interviews, she informs and guides the reader through this process, enabling twins to celebrate their individual uniqueness while taking pleasure in their twin relationship."
—Eileen M. Pearlman, PhD, Psychotherapist; Director, TwInsight;
and coauthor of Raising Twins: What Parents Want to Know
(and What Twins Want to Tell Them)

"*The Same but Different* is a real eyeopener, offering a new lens with which to view individuals who are multiples. It is a must-read not only for adult multiples but also for parents of multiple-birth children, regardless of their ages."
—Betsy Brown Braun, MA, child development and behavior specialist and
author of Just Tell Me What to Say and You're Not the Boss of Me

"A terrific book for those who find themselves thrust into twinship—one of the closest relationships imaginable but one you don't get to choose. In *The Same but Different*, you'll learn how to let go of resentment and competition, work through issues of separation and codependence, and build an honest and authentic adult relationship with your twin. Dr. Friedman, speaking with empathy, humor, and firsthand knowledge, explores a terrain that has had little light shone on it."
—Madeline Levine, PhD, author of Teach Your Children Well and
The Price of Privilege

"For those who can't access a twin specialist, Dr. Friedman provides a self-help manual that makes sense of the struggling twin's experience. A must-read for family and friends of twins."
—Audrey Sandbank, family psychotherapist and twin specialist, London, and
editor of Twin and Triplet Psychology

"Parents of identical twins do not have an easy mission. *The Same but Different* helps us better understand the feelings our children will have as adults and the importance of working with them on their own identities from early childhood. We must help them accept that although physically identical, they are independent individuals with their own unique personalities."
—Lucila Menéndez Bueno, PhD, President, AMAPAMU
(Madrid multiples parents association), and mother of
eight-year-old identical twins and a baby singleton

The Same but Different

How Twins Can Live, Love, and Learn to Be Individuals

Joan A. Friedman, PhD

ROCKY PINES PRESS

Rocky Pines Press
11870 Santa Monica Blvd., #106-666
Los Angeles, CA 90025
www.rockypinespress.com

Quantity sales. Special discounts are available on quantity purchases by corporations, associations, and others. For details, contact the "Special Sales Department" at the address above.

Orders by US trade bookstores and wholesalers. Please contact BCH: (800) 431-1579 or visit www.bookch.com for details.

Printed in the United States of America

Cataloging-in-Publication Data
    Friedman, Joan A.
        The same but different : how twins can live, love, and learn to be individuals /
    Joan A. Friedman.— First edition.
        pages cm
        Includes bibliographical references and index.
        LCCN 2013913844
        ISBN 978-0-9893464-3-6 (pbk)
        ISBN 978-0-9893464-4-3 (ebook)
        1. Twins—Psychology. I. Title.
    BF723.T9F75 2013   155.44'4
    QBI13-600138

First Edition
18 17 16 15 14   10 9 8 7 6 5 4 3 2 1

To Jane

Contents

Preface

After I wrote *Emotionally Healthy Twins*, about raising twins from infancy to young adulthood, I began to hear from adult twins who wanted to know more. They wanted to know if the struggles they were encountering as adults were related to being a twin and, if so, what they could do about their situation. Twins who came to my speaking engagements and workshops or who found me online said that they were relieved to discover that they were not alone—that other adult twins faced similar issues, such as feeling overly dependent on their twin, having trouble forging intimate relationships, worrying that one twin will feel abandoned if the other gets married or moves away, resenting the ongoing role of caretaker to their adult twin, competing with their twin's significant other, tiring of the comparisons to their twin, and wondering if they will ever be perceived and valued on their own terms.

In speaking and blogging about such concerns, treating clients in my private practice, and listening to so many adult twins eager for answers and advice, I realized that I had to write a second book. As a therapist specializing in twin issues, a mother of adult twins, and a twin myself, I knew a book was needed that specifically addresses the unique interpersonal and existential problems faced by adult twins, a group whose numbers continue to grow. According to a January 2012 report by the National Center for Health Statistics, the rate of twin births rose 76 percent from 1980 to 2009. In 2009, one out of thirty births was a twin birth.[1]

The Same but Different deals with the reality of being a twin, which bears little resemblance to the idealized portrait presented by the media. That portrait draws from what I call the *twin mystique*, which holds that twins are essentially mysterious, inseparable, and magical. Twins are assumed to be each other's predestined life partner and to feel lost without the other. They are thought to be able to read each other's minds and finish each other's sentences. Together they comprise a kind of singular entity—two as one. Such romantic assumptions thwart our understanding of what twins actually experience.

If you are a twin, as you read the stories you will identify with many of the twins' personal histories. These are women and men who have confronted and in most cases successfully dealt with the twin-related concerns we will explore throughout the book. My hope is that their stories will provide not only emotional validation but also psychological insight and meaningful guidance. Developing the capacity to be self-reflective and authentic will enhance the quality of your relationships with your twin and intimate others.

Acknowledgments

I am deeply and eternally indebted to the twins who have entrusted me with their stories and struggles. I hope that our collaboration will encourage twins to explore their relationship issues without stigma or shame.

Special thanks to Dr. Estelle Shane, "my psychological twin," whose support, admiration, and validation have helped me embrace my selfhood and intuitive intelligence.

I want to acknowledge the following people for their unconditional love, support, and encouragement: Iris Kite, Diane Worthington, Gina Osher, Laura Bellotti, Deborah Watkins, Cindy Puccio, and Lucila Melendez.

Finally, my chaotic, lively, and engaging family is the love of my life. My five adult children are terrific critical observers and avid supporters. My husband, Robert, watches over me with dutiful devotion so that I am able to complete my work without interruptions or distractions. To each of them, I am immensely grateful and appreciative.

1

Outing Your Feelings

Being a twin is a blessing and a curse. It's heaven when we get each other and hell when we don't. Our disagreements are like stab wounds. My brother can't accept that we might have a different opinion, so he'll react by saying something harsh that will just cut to the bone. I'll have a visceral feeling and just shut down. He makes me feel so guilty for not being in 100 percent agreement with him. —Jeff, 31

When Jeff talked to me about his relationship with his twin brother, Jamie, it was the first time he had ever expressed his true feelings about being and having a twin. He spoke about being unable to have a disagreement with Jamie without one of them feeling offended or crazy. He said he is unable to be himself around his brother, which he assumed was abnormal for twins. And he resents always being there for Jamie when Jamie rarely reciprocates. At the end of our initial conversation, Jeff admitted that he felt guilty for expressing such negative thoughts about the relationship that has meant more to him than any other. The anger and disappointment he had expressed to me had made him feel terribly uneasy, and he apologized for crying, saying, "I know my feelings aren't normal."

I assured him that they are.

In my many years of counseling adult twins, hundreds of women and men have confided that being a twin is a secret struggle. Secret because twins assume that their ambivalent feelings—about a relationship that others idealize—should be kept under wraps and a struggle because masking one's emotions can be stressful and traumatic. When I assure adult twins that depression, betrayal, and resentment are common responses to twin-related issues, they always express an overwhelming sense of relief. Adult same-sex twins are surprised and reassured to find out that their concerns are shared by other twins, regardless of their age or background. They are comforted when they realize that they are not alone in confronting disturbing issues stemming from one of the closest relationships imaginable yet one they didn't choose.

As you begin the self-reflective journey that this book represents, I invite you to be open with yourself about your experience of being a twin. Acknowledging conflicted or negative feelings is the first step toward understanding your twinship, discovering who you are as an individual, and deciding what you want from your relationships and your life. It wasn't that long ago that I took those initial steps myself, which led me to write this book.

Uncovering My Real Feelings about Being a Twin

My identical twin sister, Jane, and I were very close growing up. That's how we appeared to others, and that is how I characterized our relationship in my mind for many years. We were each other's favorite playmate as little girls, we enjoyed the twin celebrity status in elementary school, and we hung out together as teens. There wasn't a lot of overt conflict between us, and only years later did I discover the essential reason why we got along so well: we desperately needed each other. That need was so intense that we couldn't afford not to get along, so we became very good at avoiding conflict. The basis for our mutual neediness was rooted in our parents' inability to give us the nurturing attention we required. Embroiled in their own marital issues, they essentially left Jane and me on our own emotionally. I became Jane's loving caretaker, and she became my cherished dependent. And since we didn't really have anyone but each other, we tiptoed around any potential conflicts, unconsciously protecting our crucial connection.

After graduation from high school, Jane and I went to separate colleges, and our lives and paths began to diverge. Still, we spoke on the phone frequently, as my father attested with his complaints about the phone bills. As young adults pursuing our respective careers, we each made close friends and didn't seem to need each other as we had when we were young. Not until after we got married and had children did our unacknowledged childhood issues start to crop up.

I realized that I resented being Jane's caretaker and never getting back what I so automatically gave her: my emotional support and attentiveness. And I am certain that Jane resented my caretaking, which could come across as overbearing and intrusive. I came to understand that I had been fearful about our competitive feelings and had defended against them by keeping everything nice. Of course, we never had a hint of any of these issues when we were growing up because our authentic feelings were unknown even to ourselves.

How did I come to out these and other feelings, which had been buried throughout our childhood and young adulthood? Shortly after we were married, my husband started questioning me about how Jane and I related to each other. For instance, he wanted to know why I always seemed to defer to her and suppress how I really felt. His observations took me by surprise. I had never really thought about how Jane and I interacted. Now that our twinship seemed to be impacting my marriage, I realized I needed to take a closer look at it.

Up until then, I had seen my twin sister only from the perspective of a young twin. Jane was someone whose moods and well-being I constantly monitored. I watched out for and took care of her almost as a mother would a child, and it was a role I played from as early as I could remember. But

I did not have an accurate picture of who Jane was as an adult woman or how I authentically felt about our relationship. With the help of a therapist, I realized that although Jane and I had relied on each other as children and were connected in a unique and loving way, we had also unknowingly colluded in a kind of false closeness.

In the course of my therapy, the therapist would introduce subjects that pertained to Jane's and my relationship and ask how I felt. She would chip away at various issues, and I would respond by saying, "Are you sure?" "Really? Do you think that's true?" A part of me wanted to defend myself, Jane, and our twinship—and to deny what had really gone on between us throughout our lives.

I came to understand that my inability to see our relationship for what it was had to do with my unconscious need to maintain our twin connection. I wanted to hold on to the belief that Jane's and my feelings and responses and inclinations were exactly the same because if they weren't, according to my unconscious assumptions, our relationship would be severely threatened. Although I certainly hadn't worked this out in my mind when I was a young adult, I had operated under the principle that the only way to maintain my connection to Jane was to believe that we were identical in a very essential way—that we shared the same feelings and perceptions and that she felt toward me the way I felt toward her.

My therapist helped me understand that twins often have an ongoing wish to be the same that is in conflict with the ongoing wish to be different, and these opposing desires arise throughout life. A twin's desire to be the same as her same-age sibling in terms of feelings and perceptions is particularly persistent, which is what I had experienced with Jane. I *wanted* her to mirror my feelings and observe situations from an identical perspective, so I assumed that was the case.

Once I could accept that Jane was a unique person, with distinctly different ways of experiencing life, I was able to expand my viewpoint beyond an idealized twin perspective and see our twin dynamic much more clearly. I could acknowledge that I resented her needing my protection, and that she probably resented my caretaking. And I could finally recognize how different Jane is from me—which is how it should be. Acknowledging these truths didn't jeopardize our relationship. It offered the possibility of deepening it.

Perhaps you are struggling with the discovery of unacknowledged feelings about your relationship with your twin. Perhaps, like I once did, you tend to deny any conflicts between the two of you for fear you will upset the status quo, make matters worse, or endanger your twinship. But denying what's real rarely makes the situation better. Acknowledging that you have issues, on the other hand, can begin to shed light and create an opening for positive change.

Acknowledging Negative Feelings: An Act of Treason?

The belief that twins are intimately connected forever is so deeply embedded in our culture that when same-age siblings *don't* feel that connection, are ambivalent about maintaining it, or want to sever it and become just siblings, they often feel that something must be seriously wrong with them. In fact, such concerns about being a twin are widespread, and outing your feelings is a healthy sign that you want to acknowledge the truth about what you're experiencing.

Adult twins who contact me are grateful to finally be able to talk about their twin-related issues. Not only have they been unable to acknowledge these problems, but they also have felt that no one will understand their conflicting emotions. Given that our culture continues to cast twins in the role of enviable soul mates, an outsider may have difficulty understanding that twins sometimes feel that they don't really exist apart from their same-age sibling, that they're trapped in a quasi marriage they didn't choose, that they hate being dependent on their twin but would be lost without her or him, or that they want to break free from the one person they feel closest to. To admit such feelings can seem like treason.

Feelings of confusion, anger, and inadequacy—and even intense hostility and hatred—are common reactions twins experience and nothing to feel ashamed of. Still, many twins suffer shame and guilt when they begin to acknowledge their less-than-overjoyed feelings about being and having a twin.

Monique, an identical twin in her midtwenties, felt guilty about disclosing her feelings in our first conversation. She was distraught and angry with her twin sister, Denise, for needing her too much. Monique said she felt guilty about being so annoyed with Denise and for not wanting to be constantly "on call" for her as she had been throughout their lives. Denise called Monique every day wanting Monique to listen to her and help her figure out what to do with her life. Monique was growing increasingly impatient and was grateful to be able to talk to me about issues she had been keeping to herself for years.

"I actually feel bad that everything is going so well for me right now," Monique said. "I'm happy in my profession, I have a boyfriend I really like. But I feel bad because Denise doesn't have what I have. She lost her job, she wants a relationship but doesn't have one, and she's just very depressed—all the time. So how can I feel good about my own life when she's so down?"

Monique was not only conflicted about the discrepancies between her own life and Denise's but also about the incongruity between her love and her disdain for her twin. She was concerned about Denise and yet enraged that her sister still needed her so much. "How can I take care of myself and my own needs and yet be constantly available to help my sister?" Monique asked. "On the other hand, how can I *not* want to take care of my best friend? I feel so guilty!"

I listened to Monique express her love and resentment toward her sister and assured her that this kind of conflict and ambivalence is experienced by many adult twins. It was understandable that she resented her twin's ongoing neediness and understandable, as well, that her resentment made her feel ashamed. It was important for Monique to recognize that it is natural to have these contradictory feelings—and to work them through. I explained that if she didn't try to deal with these issues, her relationship with her sister would always be a thorn in her side, likely leaving Monique unable to move on with her other relationships.

Like so many adult twins I have counseled, Monique conveyed an enormous sense of relief at being able to out her feelings. "I've never talked about this," she said. "I've never put my thoughts together. I've never felt comfortable confronting these things. And I've never found anybody who would understand that it's not that I don't love my sister!" I told Monique that a twinship is a complicated relationship, and nontwins can find it very difficult to understand the intricacies involved in how much twins mean to each other, and yet how desperately they may yearn for independence as adolescents and as adults.

In talking with twins about their conflicted feelings, I often notice their initial disbelief that someone else actually "gets it." At first, it is as if they are saying, "Do you really understand that I don't hate my sister? Do you really understand that I love her, but I also have these dark feelings?" Once the disbelief subsides, there is a profound sense of gratitude for having their emotions validated by someone else. They then feel free to ask such questions as, how can I cope with these extreme feelings about this person that I love? How can I manage *not* to feel like a traitor to my twin?

Jeff came to me with similar questions. He felt like a traitor but had an intense need to tell somebody about how his twin brother, Jamie, irritated him and didn't understand him. "I experience things and believe things that Jamie can't possibly understand or tolerate," Jeff told me. "I've never spoken about this with anyone because not only would I feel horribly guilty about talking behind my brother's back, but I've never had a place where I could come in and talk about it and have it be understood." Knowing that I am a twin myself, that I specialize in twin issues, and that I have counseled many adult twins, Jeff felt comfortable and trusted that I could hear his complaints about his brother and understand that those grievances don't imply he is a bad person. Rather, I can understand Jeff's complaints as part of a love/hate continuum, which is common among adult twins yet rarely discussed.

While it may feel unconscionable to admit to yourself, let alone to a third party, that there are personality traits you find intolerable about your twin sibling, that you wish you could lead a more separate life, or that you resent his or her neediness, such feelings are part of the confusion that exists in many twinships. Twins fear that to harbor negative emotions toward one's alleged best friend means being disloyal to the one person most worthy of loyalty. What twins need to understand, however, is that strong feelings of love, need, and caring toward one's twin are not negated by equally strong feelings of resentment, anger, or guilt. Such emotions do not make you a traitor; they reflect a normal ambivalence that most adult twins experience and need to manage.

So why do so many twins feel they are double-crossing their same-age sibling by acknowledging negative feelings? Twins are conditioned by their families and by society into believing that being a twin is a privilege and a benefit, that it bestows a spiritual connection that will last a lifetime. And for many twin pairs, this is precisely their experience. Granted, two babies being born at the same time is a wondrous event; however, parents of twins often idealize the twinship to such an exaggerated extent that they offer no space for their twin children to express the normal sibling rivalry, competitiveness, and jostling for attention that most sisters and brothers confront in their families. While parents might admit that their twins fight, they tend to do so with a sense of surprise because they envision twins as best friends who treasure their compatibility. So when twins consider revealing to their parent that they feel stifled, irate, or bored with their same-age sibling, they worry that such revelations could be met with parental shock and distress. Parents might accuse them of being disloyal.

Perhaps you have played along with the "best friends forever" expectations of your parents and others, keeping any negative feelings under wraps.

Friends and relatives may assume that your relationship with your twin is something that it is not. So acknowledging the truth about your twinship may seem intolerable. In fact, it is a necessary step toward clarity, personal growth, and a better relationship with your twin.

Pain, Shame, and Validation

Most often what compels adult twins to contact me is that they are in pain over issues related to their twinship. They need to understand why they feel so upset or ashamed or angry—and how to rid themselves of those feelings. Maybe they have felt too ashamed of their feelings to mention the subject to anyone. Often they have lived with the emotional pain for so long that it feels almost normal, and they tell themselves that they can handle it or that circumstances will get better. The bottom line, however, is that you need to confront your feelings and understand what's going on between you and your twin before you can begin to resolve your conflicts.

One thing that often stands in the way of an adult twin outing her or his feelings to a therapist is a sense of shame that her twin connection feels uncomfortably constricting. Clients have said they feel embarrassed to come out and say they hate the fact that their twin is still so dependent on them. In a certain way this confession is similar to a mother venting to a therapist, "I'm sick of being a mother! I don't want to take care of my child anymore, but I feel so guilty for even thinking that!" Many twins often feel guilty that they, too, want to sever their caretaking role. They have been taught to believe that it is their obligation to take care of their twin sister or brother, but they are tired of being saddled with that obligation because it is seriously interfering with their own quality of life.

If you and your twin have remained locked in a synergetic relationship for a long time, you may feel so ashamed of your ultracloseness that to out such feelings can take real courage. Such was the case with forty-five-year-old Glenn. Glenn was grateful to talk to a fellow twin (me) about his predicament because he was embarrassed about the extent to which he and his brother Gary were emotionally tied together, or *enmeshed*. He had never revealed this to anyone, but Glenn confided that he felt his body "tingling" whenever his brother was upset. He would get an actual physical reaction to news that his brother was going through even a relatively minor difficulty. The level of his enmeshment with Gary was so profound that Glenn felt he would be ridiculed for admitting it. But he was finally compelled to make an appointment with me because his brother was falling apart, there was nothing Glenn could do to help him, and he could no longer tolerate his feelings of helplessness. Glenn was worried and concerned for his brother's well-being but also terribly angry—because nothing he was doing was putting his brother back together again.

I told Glenn that it made perfect sense that he felt angry; after all, he and his brother—because they are twins—had been made to feel responsible for each other's happiness throughout their lives. Who *wouldn't* feel angry about continually bearing the burden of looking after someone whom you love but cannot "fix" or make happy? Why *wouldn't* you feel angry that you aren't allowed to focus on your own life and be responsible solely for yourself, as a nontwin is allowed to do?

It also was understandable that Glenn was ashamed of his overly close relationship with his twin. Singletons would rarely be so devoted to a sibling, or become so extremely upset by every troubling event in a brother or sister's life—especially at age forty-five. To exhibit such extreme emotions can be humiliating, even for a twin, whom society expects will care about a same-age sibling as a spouse would his mate. Being held hostage by the emotional neediness of his brother was indeed a shameful situation for Glenn.

And, of course, his feelings of shame and anger were causing Glenn a great deal of emotional pain. How could it be any other way, when those feelings were largely suppressed and unexamined?

What Glenn realized in our initial meetings was that the pain and shame were understandable—and normal. It was comforting for him to know this, to have his feelings finally authenticated. Validation of such troubling and ongoing emotions became a launchpad to Glenn's journey of self-discovery, individuation, and independence.

Breaking Through the Twin Mystique

Why does outing your feelings about your twin often seem so difficult—as if you were violating a taboo? I believe the fundamental reason is that our culture idealizes and romanticizes twins. We are perceived not simply as individuals who are born at the same time, but as mystical creatures who shared a womb and will forever share an unfathomable intimacy. Most people think of twins as intensely close soul mates connected to each other through a kind of sibling ESP. Many assume that one twin not only knows what the other is thinking and feeling but also can make up for any deficiencies in the other's persona. Twins are seen as inhabiting their own private world. It is assumed that they feel lost without the other and that they seek to preserve their twosome status even as adults. Nontwins fantasize that in a twin relationship one always knows what the other one wants and needs; this creates a sense that twins are each other's predestined partner and confidant.

Each of these assumptions contributes to what I call *the twin mystique*. There is something inherently captivating about the idea of having a double because it invokes a human longing for an intimate, lifelong companion who thoroughly understands his or her partner. People believe that with such a companion, one would never be abandoned or alone. Nontwins project this longing onto twins and see them as enjoying a magical, intermingled relationship.

In fact, twins *can* be lifelong friends, and they can fulfill many emotional needs for each other. But if they are expected to fulfill the fantasy of telepathic soul mates who inhabit their own world, they will never feel free to develop as truly separate people. When the longing to see twins in a romanticized way prevents others from seeing same-age siblings as individuals, twins feel as if they are merely playing a role in someone else's fantasy.

And then there are the cultural references that further embellish the romantic notion of hyperconnected, indivisible twins. In the film *The Social Network*, identical twins Cameron and Tyler Winklevoss go up against Facebook creator Mark Zuckerberg for allegedly stealing their idea. Before they take their case to their lawyers, the brothers consider punching out Zuckerberg. Attempting to convince his brother that Zuckerberg will be easy to defeat, one twin says, "I'm six-foot-five, 220 pounds—and there are two of me." The remark gets a laugh from the audience and reinforces the notion that twins are essentially clones. The actual Winklevoss twinship is further embellished in a *Washington Post* article, in which the writer states that "The real Winklevosses have recently completed matching MBAs at Oxford."[2] Matching MBAs? It is as if the writer even wants to depict the brothers' academic accomplishments as identical—or at least in sync. In fact, Tyler Winklevoss seems to think of himself as quite distinct from his brother. When asked by a reporter if he thought he looked like the actor who played him, he replied, "Asking a twin that question is funny because we're used to seeing the smallest differences between each other."[3]

The media often portray twins as an awesome duo—a more potent force than a mere singular character, given their double identity. Whether they're aligned with the good guys or the forces of evil, twins are thought to deliver twice the wallop, and thus their presence in literature and film is both exotic and thrilling. One charming set of twins currently appealing to younger audiences is the Weasley Twins in the *Harry Potter* books and movies. Mischievous and creative, Fred and George Weasley are said to fight tyranny and hatred with their clever sense of humor and daring sense of adventure. Their personalities are described as very similar, yet completely opposite from their older brother, Percy. According to their younger sister, Ginny, "The thing about growing up with Fred and George is that you sort of start thinking anything's possible if you've got enough nerve."[4] It is clear that two Weasleys provide at least twice the fun and excitement than either would on his own.

Embodying the evil side of the twin spectrum is the twin brother and sister team, Jane and Alec, in the *Twilight Saga* book and film series. Imbued with magnificent, sadistic powers, they are considered to be the Volturi's most offensive weapons. Each twin possesses the ability to crush an opponent, earning themselves the moniker "the witch twins."[5]

On a slightly more realistic level, Phoebe, the loveable yet quirky character on the television series *Friends*, has an identical twin named Ursula whose outrageous, bad girl behavior is mistaken for Phoebe's. In one instance, Phoebe receives unwanted attention from men until she discovers that Ursula is starring in pornographic films using Phoebe's name. In another episode, Ursula sells Phoebe's birth certificate to a Swedish runaway. Such twin antics reinforce the notion that having an identical twin provides the perfect opportunity for devious schemes and trickery. And the Phoebe/Ursula twinship also bolsters the idea of the good twin/bad twin dichotomy, a notion that is apparent in popular culture.

The double whammy threat of the Winklevoss whiz kids, the dual charms of Harry Potter's buddies, and the underhanded pranks of a Friend's conniving twin—each stereotype plays into and fortifies the twin mystique. Enjoying such portrayals as entertainment is fine, but when it comes to your own behavior, breaking through the twin mystique means rejecting cultural expectations and, instead, honoring your individual feelings and your right to an individual life.

Getting Comfortable with Ambivalence

Honoring your individual feelings about your twinship may sound like a straightforward assignment, but for many twins it can be daunting. That's because recognizing both the positive and negative parts of your relationship contradicts what twins are often taught. Having minor squabbles with your twin may be okay when you're young, but as adults, twins are generally expected to appreciate and treasure their twin and the twinship. Thanks to the twin mystique, many twins feel they aren't entitled to a more nuanced, ambivalent perspective on their relationship. They believe they must live up to the expectation that twins only recognize the best in each other and are essentially on the same page. With the standard set so high, a twin may sense that any negative feeling toward his or her same-age sibling has the power to destroy the twinship. But are twin relationships really that fragile—or can adult twins be truthful about how they feel without fearing it will be the end of the world?

The key to a healthy twinship is becoming comfortable integrating two opposing emotions that you might feel toward your twin. Handling ambivalence means allowing contradictory feelings to surface and realizing that, when you do, you'll be better equipped to deal with problems in your relationship. A prerequisite for healthy attachment is the ability to hold both loving and upset emotions toward someone. When you can acknowledge reasonable negative feelings without the fear of destroying the relationship, you position yourself to engage more authentically and deeply with those to whom you're closest.

Perhaps your interactions with your twin often leave you feeling frustrated, overwhelmed, or excessively disappointed. Learning to feel comfortable with ambivalence means that you can accept such unpleasant feelings as a natural consequence of your connection to your twin, just as your love for him or her is also natural. The more comfortable you become with such mixed emotions, the less guilty you're likely to be when you acknowledge and express your negative feelings.

Nora, a lively and insightful twenty-five-year-old, struggled to articulate and understand her authentic, yet conflicting, feelings toward her twin sister, Lynette: resentment, guilt, and love. "I never thought there was any problem with my relationship with my twin sister," Nora told me in an interview.

We were pretty much inseparable during grammar school; we were put in separate classes but went to the same birthday parties and had the same friends. Then at college we roomed together and socialized together, but I started having more friends of my own. Usually, though, I'd ask them if it was okay if Lynette joined us—not because I wanted her there necessarily but because I knew she was shy and had a hard time making friends. It wasn't until we graduated college and I was working and living on my own, about ten miles from her, that I noticed this kind of nagging feeling whenever Lynette would call me during the week and ask what I was doing on the weekend. I could hear in her voice that she was lonely and wanted me to fill in that void for her. My chest would tighten, and I knew I couldn't just go about my life without her.

But I really just wanted to *not* have to worry about her for once. We were both all grown up now, and I wanted to finally do my thing, be my own person. But I felt so sorry for her, that I absolutely couldn't abandon her. And that part of me that felt uncomfortable and angry. I tried to just stuff it down—until I kind of blew up at her one time about something totally unrelated to anything. With the help of a therapist, I started looking at my relationship with Lynette and realizing that these feelings of *not* wanting her around all the time were beginning to get to me. Now, sometimes anyway, I can say no to my sister when I don't want to be with her, and I feel okay about it. There's still a twinge of guilt, but I'm understanding more that it is okay to disappoint her. It doesn't mean I don't love her.

Unfortunately, most twins don't feel they have permission to express what they authentically feel about being and having a twin. Many fear that to do so would mean jeopardizing a relationship that is often valued even more highly than a marriage. Sadly, when your honest feelings about your twinship are suppressed, what is presumed to be the most intimate of relationships becomes one of the most inauthentic and dishonest. Rather than acknowledging any negative feelings toward your twin, you may either put up a good front or constantly argue without getting to the root of what's bothering you. Whether your twinship is superficially compatible or outwardly combative, neither extreme can reflect the spectrum of your authentic feelings. Every close relationship involves ambivalence, and this is especially true of twins who may feel they must live up to the unrealistic expectation of lifelong closeness and sanctioned codependency. Given such intense pressure to match the twin ideal, the very real connection most twins feel, and the inevitable conflicts that arise, it is no wonder that adult twins feel a mixture of resentment and love, guilt and loyalty, anger and delight.

When you become comfortable with ambivalence, you can abandon the simplistic belief that adult twins must be either perfectly matched soul mates or fractured enemies—and begin to believe in the healing power of emotional truth.

Rocking the Emotional Boat

By rocking the boat I don't necessarily mean outing your feelings to your twin or to a therapist, although you may decide to do so at some point. I am talking about being honest with yourself about how you feel toward your twin and the relationship the two of you have shared throughout your lives. Giving yourself permission to acknowledge your true feelings is incredibly liberating. Finally being able to say to yourself, "I'm angry at my twin for holding me back from what I really want to do" or "I'm fed up with needing my twin too much," will be a first step toward setting yourself free from the constraints of an unhealthy, binding relationship. But freeing yourself cannot happen without emotional honesty.

When you hide your feelings from yourself, you restrict your ability to know yourself and authentically relate to others. Unacknowledged emotions spill over into your interactions not only with your twin but others as well, so that you react to people without understanding your reactions. Keeping secrets becomes a breeding ground for confusion, distortion, and misperceptions. You may get intensely irritated or upset but are unable to trace your emotions to the feelings hidden in that twinship boat, which you don't want to rock for fear of capsizing. The truth is that you cannot be authentic with anyone if you're not in touch with your emotional core, and for twins that core includes the person who was born on your birthday.

Being afraid to confront your true feelings about your twinship is understandable because doing so is a signal that you're ready to make a change, and change is scary. Although you may be apprehensive about confronting the truth, facing your twinship issues and working through them will be immensely liberating. You'll discover you have the option to release yourself from the stereotypic ways that twins are forced to relate to each other. You'll be able to choose the type of relationship you'd like to have with your twin brother or sister. And you'll feel that you deserve to live your life as a singular adult, rather than as half of a duo. You'll gain perspective on yourself and your twin so that you can enjoy each other as friends and siblings rather than idealized partners. And you'll understand that your adult relationships don't have to replicate your twinship.

Rocking the emotional boat doesn't require that you and your twin "tell all" to one another; you can certainly keep your revelations and insights to yourself. What it does require is giving yourself permission to recognize the troubling emotions you've been carrying in that boat so you can deal with them in a beneficial way—and get on with your life.

If outing your feelings is step one, what's next? The process of acknowledging, exploring, and dealing with your twinship issues can be summed up in these essential steps:

1. Rock the emotional boat by outing your feelings.

2. Explore those feelings—either on your own (in conjunction with this book) or with a therapist who is familiar with twin issues.

3. Deal with your twin-related feelings and issues so that you feel free to pursue the life you choose.

Throughout this book, we'll be discussing the most common issues that arise between identical and nonidentical same-sex twins. Certainly every relationship is unique, but many twins face similar emotional hurdles. As you identify those issues that most closely resemble yours and learn how others have confronted and dealt with them, you'll begin to discover what you can do to improve your twinship—and flourish in your own life.

Adult Twin Survey

I invite you to read through the following list of survey statements and identify any concerns and feelings that you share. This will help you to recognize your particular issues so you'll be better prepared to address them throughout the book. Reviewing these statements will also help you to realize that you are not alone in feeling many of the distressing emotions you may have been reluctant to acknowledge.

☐ I'll never love anyone as much as my twin, and that worries me.

☐ I've never had the chance to figure out who I am apart from my twin.

☐ I would be lost if my twin moved to another city.

☐ I feel guilty for wishing that my twin lived somewhere else so that I could be more independent from her/him.

☐ I don't know how to tell my twin that I need more space without hurting her/his feelings.

☐ I can't concentrate on my own life because I'm constantly worried about my twin's well-being.

☐ I feel guilty for not wanting to introduce my friends to my twin for fear I'll have to share them with her/him.

☐ I feel resentful that I can't achieve what I know I'm capable of, because I don't want to outshine my twin.

☐ I am often disappointed in my friends because they don't match up to my relationship with my twin.

☐ I feel hurt that my twin shuts me out of his/her life.

☐ I get very depressed when I think of how my twin and I have grown apart.

☐ I get extremely upset when my twin expresses an opinion that's so opposite of mine. It feels like we're no longer connected.

☐ I can't be straight with my twin and tell her/him how I really feel about our relationship.

☐ I always feel that I'm competing with my twin, and this holds me back from what I really want to accomplish.

☐ I feel like I have to fake feeling closer to my twin than I actually feel.

☐ I hate it when my twin tells me how he/she wants us always to be as close as we were when we were kids. That's not how I feel at all, but I can't tell her/him that.

☐ I wish I had never been born a twin.

☐ I'm envious of nontwins who enjoy a more normal relationship with their siblings.

☐ My boyfriend/girlfriend/spouse resents how close I am with my twin, and I don't know what to do about it.

☐ I feel ashamed that I don't want my twin to feel closer to his/her partner than he/she feels toward me.

☐ It bothers me that my twin doesn't approve of my choice in partners, and I worry that I'm too influenced by his/her opinions.

☐ I think my relationship with my boyfriend/girlfriend/spouse would be much better if I didn't have to worry about my twin.

☐ I'm constantly disappointed in the partners I choose because these relationships don't compare to the closeness I feel with my twin.

☐ I feel ashamed of how much I still need my twin; I want to let go, but I'm terrified to be without his/her emotional support.

☐ I feel guilty for hoping that my twin will replace me with someone else.

2

Twin Closeness— Assumptions and Realities

I feel better when I do things without my twin. This is not to say that I don't enjoy doing things with her, but somehow when she is not there I feel more like myself. I love her, but I just feel smothered around her. By myself I can be myself. —Brianna, 18

I get along with my twin, but it's kinda like being with a copycat or wanna-be version of myself. —Noah, 23

I think my husband is glad that I have my close relationship with my twin sister because he cannot meet my emotional needs the way she does. —Eileen, 45

What does it mean to be close to a sister or brother? For most people, it means enjoying family experiences and memories, being able to be yourself around each other, sharing how you feel, and being there for one another in times of need. While a close relationship with your sibling is something to value, not all sisters and brothers are close as children, and many are not at all close as adults. When that's the case, it is considered a shame but not a tragedy.

For twins, however, the expectations are a lot higher. Due to the beliefs implicit in the twin mystique, many assume that throughout their lives, twins will feel closer to each other than to anyone else. Some take for granted that twins will enjoy a closer relationship with each other than with their parents, friends, other siblings, or even their mates. Such devoted intimacy does exist for a great many twins; however, many others experience their twinship quite differently.

In this chapter we're going to explore how the ultraclose relationship thought to be the norm for adult twins doesn't always gel with reality. What may feel like closeness to one twin can feel like overdependence to the other. The stories in this chapter reveal a spectrum of twinship experiences: some adult twins feel unable to get their needs met by anyone other than their twin; others feel frustrated by their desire to be more independent from their twin; some feel inauthentic for faking a closeness with their twin that they don't really feel; still others are seeking a balance between connection to and separation from their twin. Wherever you place yourself on the closeness continuum, this chapter will help you assess how comfortable you are with your own level of twin closeness and what changes you might want to consider.

Twin Closeness: Choice or Obligation?

When twins have been raised as individuals, they experience their relationship as quite similar to that of singleton siblings—with perhaps a deepened connection due to their identical age. While they are likely to enjoy a close companionship, same-age siblings raised as unique individuals perceive themselves as separate from their twin. Their primary attachment is to their parents, not to their twin, so as children they receive essential parental nurturing and caretaking, which then enables them to develop a "self" apart from their twin. They may choose each other as playmates (and later on as best friends) when they're at home or at school, but they feel free to develop their own friendships without any sense of obligation to include their twin.

In families where twins have not been given the chance to define themselves as separate from each other, they often grow up in a relationship that resembles a dysfunctional marriage. In such cases, parents have likely abdicated their role as primary nurturer, giving over that function, sometimes unconsciously, to the twins, who are expected to care for each other both physically and emotionally. Parents may also instill in their same-age children the notion that one's twin is an automatic "mate," and the twinship is thus based on pleasing—and expecting to be pleased by—one's twin. This may sound idyllic to nontwins, but when one is solely focused on either pleasing or being pleased by the other person, one lacks experience in pleasing oneself. It then becomes nearly impossible to discover one's true likes and dislikes or what it means to be authentically close to someone. Twin closeness may be experienced as an obligation, not a choice. You are close to one another because that is your expected role. And unlike marriage, not only have you not chosen this "mate," but you are placed in a quasi marriage before you are old enough to know who you are as an individual. So the "marriage" precedes your own development and is based upon someone else's expectations, not on your own emotions or proclivities.

In such a twin-defined bubble, you learn at a very young age to accommodate and compromise. Your perspective is that of a twin couple, so that you habitually think of yourself in relationship to your twin. You may find that you are in constant collusion—enabling, accommodating, and codepending on each other—rather than feeling free to act on your own or make your own decisions.

This is not to say that all twinships are either one type or the other: "twins-as-a-couple" or "two completely distinct individuals." You may consider yourself very much an individual, yet sometimes your behavior may be influenced by how it will impact your twin. And twinships very often change over time. A twin "couple" may find that their relationship changes significantly when one goes off to college in another city, becomes involved with a partner, or gets married.

Still, it can be difficult to alter a pattern that has been in place throughout your lives, even when you desire change between you and your twin. Fundamental to making desired changes is to understand what type of relationship you have with your sibling. Is your closeness based on choice and rooted in your secure, individual identities? Or are there elements of codependence and enmeshment in your twinship, so that sometimes you worry that without your twin you don't really feel whole?

Codependence and Enmeshment versus Authentic Closeness

Codependency is often used to refer to a particular dynamic found in couples. It includes the tendency to be passive or overly caretaking in ways that negatively impact the relationship and the partners' quality of life. And it involves giving one's own needs a lesser priority while being excessively preoccupied with the needs of another person.[6]

As it pertains to twinship, codependency can be defined as each twin being dependent on the other to fulfill a particular role or function. In fulfilling these functions for one another, each sibling has a sense of purpose; however, with this shared dependence as a constant, neither twin is likely to learn how to perform the other person's functions for him- or herself. Psychotherapist and author Audrey C. Sandbank refers to this dynamic in terms of "allocation of tasks":

> Tasks can be emotional as well as practical. One partner may make friends and bring them home, while the other may be more cautious. They may inhibit such skills developing in the other twin . . . They become like two pieces of a jigsaw puzzle, each needing the other to become complete.[7]

Because codependent twins need and depend upon each other to feel complete and to define who they are, neither sibling is able to attain an individual sense of self.

Enmeshment refers to the blurring of boundaries between individuals such that one feels one does not really exist without the other, that one has no "self" without the other person. The term enmeshment derives from family systems theory and describes a condition in which "two or more people weave their lives and identities around one another so tightly that it is difficult for any one of them to function independently."[8]

In a twin relationship, this is evidenced in the need to maintain sameness and equality because any differences between the two siblings are seen as a threat to the two-as-one entity. There is the sense that one cannot live without the other and that one does not exist without the other twin's constant presence. Outside relationships—friends, lovers, or spouses—are often seen as a potential threat to the duo, unless the friends are equally shared and the spouses can accept that the twinship takes precedence over the marriage. Enmeshed twins tend to have little capacity for self-reflection and lack the emotional space required to consider their own choices, desires, and needs. Carving out such space for themselves entails confronting the fear that they might forever alienate their twin, with whom their life is so closely intertwined.

Given these descriptions of overly involved twinships, what might an authentic, healthy closeness look like? Ideally, it would reflect two distinct individuals, each with a secure sense of self, who keep in touch and get together because they care about each other and enjoy each other's company. Their relationship would be based on choice, not need. As mentioned earlier, such healthy twin relationships are most often the result of secure attachments to the parents during childhood and adequate opportunities for each twin to discover his unique self, apart from his twin. However, even if this has not been the case, adult twins can still develop a healthy closeness. If, for example, twins acknowledge that theirs is a codependent relationship, each can make a commitment to understand how their twinship has functioned so far and work toward cultivating an individual identity. As each sibling develops a distinct sense of self, he or she is able to embrace the twinship out of caring and love rather than insecurity and need. In turn, the twinship becomes flexible and resilient enough to tolerate other important attachments in each twin's life, without feelings of abandonment or resentment.

The Closeness Continuum

The following stories highlight the issue of closeness within twin relation-ships and how feeling closely connected to one's sibling is often confused with codependence and enmeshment. The first story reveals the struggle of a young woman who feels lost without her twin sister but realizes she must create an independent life for herself, something her twin has already done. The second focuses on two overly involved sisters who cannot seem to live with or without each other. The third shows how twins can remain so closely connected that the prospect of differentiating themselves seems both threatening and unbearable. And finally, the last story shows how a healthy closeness between twins can develop in adulthood and is reflected in each sibling's individuality, authenticity, and ability to enjoy her twin's company without needing her to feel complete.

"I'm Afraid of Losing Her"—Gina's Story

At twenty, Gina is struggling to discover who she is apart from her twin sister, Priscilla. Gina is a college junior and feels lost without the sister on whom she depended until high school, when family circumstances forced them apart. (Gina moved in with their mother, while Priscilla remained with their father.) But while Gina has been on her own for years, she still longs for the companionship and guidance she once enjoyed with her twin. She offers several reasons why friendships with other people would be not only pointless but virtually impossible. First of all, she claims that friendships with others would pale in comparison: "I don't have the desire to be as close to anyone as I am to my twin sister because I know that no one understands me like she does. I don't even want to waste my time getting frustrated by trying to explain what I mean or how I feel about a particular situation to a friend because I don't have to do that with my twin sister." Gina also claims that making new friends would seriously jeopardize her relationship with her sister: "If I have other best friends," she said, "my bonds to my twin will weaken and I will lose her." And finally, she holds back from making new friends due to her professed social anxiety, which had been ameliorated by Priscilla's presence:

> I just feel that I never say the right thing, that I've lost the ability to talk to people, or make a good impression on people. Priscilla was always able to make up for what I lack, for what I couldn't say or do. She could put into words what I meant, and without her I just feel like I can't express myself properly so I don't say anything. I'm afraid to open up so I cut myself off from potential friendships.

Interestingly, during our conversation, Gina expressed herself beautifully and was articulate, animated, and insightful. But after years of acceding to her sister's willingness to "talk for both of us," Gina is convinced that her sister was much more capable of communicating for her than Gina is of communicating for herself. "Priscilla could express what I felt and did it so much better—and I was happy for her to take over," she said. So she holds on to this alleged handicap as part of her rationale for not pursuing new friendships, which then becomes a kind of self-fulfilling prophecy.

Gina's longing to be more closely connected to her sister is definitely one-sided, a fact of which she is painfully aware. Priscilla is doing fine on her own, and Gina admits that "It sometimes hurts me because she doesn't act as bothered by not having me around all the time. It seems like her life hasn't skipped a beat compared to mine, which I feel is in shambles without her." While it is true that Priscilla is happily proceeding with her life, that doesn't mean she doesn't want a close relationship with Gina. She constantly reassures Gina that they will be connected no matter what. But connection and dependence are not the same.

I told Gina that there is a profound difference between a close sibling connection and a dependent relationship, which is what she experienced with her sister throughout their childhood. Due to problems between their parents and their parents' inability to be there for their daughters emotionally, the girls turned to each other for nurturing. In addition to their twin dependency, the girls witnessed repeatedly how much their mother constantly relied on men for her sense of self-worth. So theirs was a family where everyone was codependent, and there was no role model for healthy relationships.

As they matured in their teens, Priscilla was able to break free from her dependence on the twinship but Gina was not. Gina had never fully experienced herself as an individual, as someone who existed apart from her sister, even when they were forced to live apart. She told herself she needed her twin to complete her and never learned how to own her feelings or experiences. Learning to speak for herself, even if such attempts might seem awkward or stilted at first, would be a worthwhile challenge in making friends and getting involved in healthy relationships.

I explored with Gina how relinquishing her dependence on Priscilla will necessitate getting in touch with and fulfilling her own needs. Holding on to her sister out of desperation will not insure a close connection, but could in fact threaten it.

"We Have This Anger toward Each Other; Where Does It Stem From?"—Fiona and Paulina

Fiona and Paulina, college graduates in their midtwenties, have both moved back home with their parents. Like many young adults whose jobs don't yet afford them the ability to live on their own, both women feel frustrated about still being under the influence of their parents. What exasperates them further is their relationship to one another. They rely on each other as a married couple would; but unlike a married couple, theirs is not a committed relationship that they chose as consenting adults. Rather, they have been counting on each other since they were children in ways that they now take for granted but also resent.

In speaking with Paulina and Fiona separately, I learned that Fiona resents being the one who is obligated to make the social plans, which always have to include Paulina. If she fails to invite Paulina, their mother gets angry at Fiona, demanding to know why she didn't ask Paulina to go with her. Since Paulina recently broke up with a boyfriend and has been feeling depressed, Fiona feels sorry for her and relents. But the resentment builds.

For her part, Paulina feels she does her share of looking after Fiona's needs, such as reminding her to get her driver's license renewed. "She expects things of me," Paulina says, "like she'll say, 'You're doing it for yourself, so why wouldn't you tell me to get my license renewed?' And then she'll call me selfish because I thought about it but I didn't tell her. So I said, 'You're a human being, don't you look at your driver's license that expires on our birthday? Can't you think for yourself?' Those kinds of things bother me. I'm more responsible, and she expects me to take care of that part of her life."

Again, from Fiona's perspective, Paulina is the one who needs constant "baby-sitting":

> She likes to "sulk" in her own worries. I'm just tired of it. We've had enough of each other. I got a television for my room—she doesn't have one in her room. So she's in my room every night, and half the time she falls asleep in my bed, and I'm like, "Please leave. Please leave my room. I just want to be by myself tonight. Is that so much to ask?" She'll say, "You're such a bitch, why are you kicking me out?" and I'll say, "Because I need to be by myself. You need to understand that I need my time." But she gets really offended that I tell her to leave. And I go, "Look, I'm not telling you because I hate you. I love you, but I just need to be by myself." She doesn't understand.

A simple request to have one's room to oneself should be easy for a twenty-four-year-old sibling to understand, but Paulina and Fiona have been thrown together throughout their lives, so that feeling entitled to her own space seems foreign to Fiona, even though not having that space becomes exasperating. The cycle goes something like this: Fiona becomes frustrated with Paulina's behavior; she calls her on it; they argue; Fiona feels guilty and either gives in to Paulina or laughs it off; Fiona's resentment grows. In describing this pattern, Fiona seemed at a loss about how to break it.

> I would love for you to help me. So much of how we are together bothers me. For instance, when we're going out together, it feels like I'm always pulling her along. We were supposed to have dinner with our girlfriends the other night, the reservation was at eight, and she decides to take a shower at 8 o'clock. It drives me nuts! So I just left the house. I used to wait for her, but I don't wait anymore because I'll be late and my friends will say, "Why are you late?" and I'll just answer "Paulina" . . . and it bothers me. I shouldn't have to threaten her, constantly be on top of her, checking in on her. She's not my husband. She's not my partner. Why should I constantly have to oversee her? I need to worry about myself!

I told Fiona that she and Paulina have been playing off each other throughout their lives, so there must be something that Fiona gets from telling Paulina what to do. I asked, "If you didn't have that powerful effect on Paulina, how do you think you'd feel?" Fiona said that she would feel good.

> I wouldn't feel stressed or annoyed or irritated. Honestly, it is really annoying. I feel like I have to baby-sit her. For instance, when we go out she sometimes acts bitchy with our friends. I was growing to hate her for this, and I didn't want to hate her. So I just distanced myself a lot from her. I would go out with my other friends and I kind of wouldn't tell her. I would just kind of do my own thing. I need my own space, but I can't tell her I need it because she's going to hate me if I tell her, "I need space from you." So I kind of did my own thing for a while, and that was kind of good—I kind of had my own space and I really needed it. I felt like she was too much in my space.

There is a great deal of equivocating in Fiona's statement. She "kind of" did her own thing, but she couldn't bring herself to tell Paulina that she needs her own space. She recognizes that she needs her own life and the distance from her sister, but she can't be straightforward with Paulina about it. I told Fiona that her fear of hurting Paulina's feelings is doing more harm than good. By refusing to set boundaries with her sister that would allow for her own needs to be met, Fiona is preventing both sisters from breaking the dynamic of codependency. Paulina is dependent on Fiona not only for scheduling social activities but for keeping her in line emotionally, as a toddler is dependent on a mother. And Fiona goes along with such caretaking because she is dependent on Paulina as well. Fiona's well-being is contingent on Paulina feeling okay and not having her feelings hurt. Helping Paulina to allegedly feel better provides Fiona with a degree of power over her sister, which, though unacknowledged, Fiona depends upon.

Unfortunately, this unhealthy dynamic keeps the sisters in a constant state of bickering because neither one really wants to be dependent on the other, but neither knows how to break free from the cycle. Paulina confessed, "My sister and I have these issues, we argue, and we have this anger with each other, but I don't even know where it stems from."

In order for the sisters to break the cycle of codependency, they need to understand what causes their anger and fights. Fiona and Paulina's codependency began early on. Their parents believed (and still do) in the sanctity of twinship and that the girls should be together as much as possible, so that is how they were raised. Given little opportunity to be on their own, they grew to depend on each other and yet to resent their lack of freedom and independence. While a lot of positives exist in their relationship—being there for each other, having fun together—it is no wonder that their anger derives from never having had their own space in which to develop their individuality. Fiona related that one of the best times in her life was a vacation she took with college girlfriends. Her parents tried to convince her to take Paulina along, but Fiona insisted that this was her time with her friends. "I had to beg my parents not to buy Paulina a ticket to come," Fiona said, "but it's the best thing I ever did. It was so much fun."

I explained to Fiona and Paulina that in a codependent relationship, both individuals are angry. The person who is dependent is angry because she doesn't really want to be dependent on someone else but can't seem to extricate herself from a position of dependency, and the person who is in control also feels angry because she doesn't want the burden of having someone dependent on her but can't let the other person be on her own for fear that something terrible might happen. So both parties are locked in an ongoing scenario in which anger and frustration rule their relationship. With twins, codependency is likely a dynamic that has existed since childhood, so it is that much more difficult to undo. In Fiona and Paulina's case, Fiona cannot imagine how Paulina will survive without her protection. She hates having to include her in all her social plans and resents having to kick her out of her room at night so that she can have some space to herself. But she continues to defend Paulina's neediness, only to state in the next breath that she feels it is unfair that she has to constantly hold her hand. Her parents' demand that she take care of Paulina only makes matters worse. All of this emotional turmoil leaves Fiona feeling she has no viable course of action:

> I feel bad because Paulina doesn't have anyone to hang out with. And if I don't tell her to come, then she'll have no one to hang out with, and then my parents are going to say, "Why don't you tell Paulina to come with you, she's home alone." Well I don't want her to come with me! Why do I always have to hold her hand?

I told Fiona that the bottom line is this: if she doesn't start standing up for her own needs, she will be crippling herself and her sister. Fiona is enabling Paulina's dependence, ensuring that Paulina will be tied forever to her sister's coattails. By failing to draw a boundary between her life and

Paulina's, Fiona is allowing Paulina to stay stuck in a forced reliance that she likely detests. But one of them needs to make the first move.

I explained (to both of them) that setting physical boundaries is an initial step. A physical separation—declaring their own rooms off bounds to the other, going out separately with friends—can then grow into a psychological and emotional separation. Fiona can tell Paulina, "I need time to myself in my own room" or "I need the freedom to be with my friends on my own." And Paulina can create her own ground rules: "I need you to be responsible for your own documents and paperwork (for example, remind yourself to get your license renewed)." When Fiona and Paulina can be consistent in setting their own boundaries, their behavior will change—and so will their dynamic.

Fiona confided that she didn't enjoy trying to manage her sister's life and was fed up with the constant arguments and squabbling. She was definitely ready to give up a role she didn't really choose:

> When I tell her what to do, it kind of gives me power but a big part of me doesn't want to have that power. And it's at the expense of myself—like additional stress and anxiety. It is so frustrating for me. I don't want to be like a Nazi—I really don't. It's not fun for me.

A nontwin who does not understand how an overly dependent twin-ship can cause such rifts might get the impression that Paulina and Fiona have little love for each other, that it has been driven away by antagonism and conflict. But that would be the wrong impression. Here are comments from each sister describing their closeness even in the context of their current troubles. Fiona said:

> When we have good times, it's great. We bond over how annoyed we are with our parents, or what one of our friends said or did. We can sit and talk for hours. But she has to know when she's crossing the line with me. That's what it is.

Paulina added:

I'm lucky to have had her because we share a bond that nobody else would ever have. It is comforting to have her there, but there are also times when I just want to say, "I want you away from me!"

I assured Paulina and Fiona that their sisterly bond will not be broken when each of them learns to be less dependent on the other and begins to develop her own sense of self. In fact, I believe their relationship will be strengthened once they break free from their pattern of codependency. They will then be able to enjoy each other's company without the oppressive feelings of resentment, anger, and insecurity.

"I'd Rather Be Dependent and Happy Than Independent and Unhappy"—Grace and Victoria

Like many twins, Grace's and Victoria's voices sound remarkably alike. Interviewing them on the phone, it was hard to tell them apart, but what came across most vividly wasn't the similarity of their voices so much as how startlingly identical their opinions were about their twinship, their jobs, their plans for the future. Enthusiastic, thoughtful, and devoted—to their career, their religious faith, and each other—they seemed as delighted with their relationship as any two siblings could be. Grace and Victoria are in their early twenties. They live together and even share the same job since their professional backgrounds are so similar. They describe the work arrangement as a godsend.

Victoria said:

> We were both looking for the same type of job—and I managed to
> see this job-share opening. So it was just perfect, like a sign from God
> that we could have the same job.

Grace commented:

> And now that we've got the same job, we say that we couldn't do
> it without each other, really. And we wouldn't be able to live here
> without each other because it would just be really, really lonely.

In the last several years, each sister had to endure the occasional lone-liness of being without the other, but both insisted they do not wish to repeat that experience. Grace explained:

> We didn't live together at university, but we lived in flats next door to each other. And then in my last year, Victoria graduated one year before me—because I had to change my course—so I had an extra year at university. I was there without her for a year, which was really hard. She came to see me all the time.

Victoria added:

> I recently lived on my own for about six months with a family that I didn't know, and I was really independent. And now since living with her again, it's like I've become more dependent on her. And I don't really like doing things on my own. It's a bit worrying because it is like a step backwards. But all that time for those six months I really missed her. And I'm just so happy that she's here now that I don't really care that I'm not independent because I'd rather be dependent and happy than independent and unhappy.

So what could be the downside in being so ultraconnected to one's twin, given that the close connection seems to make both siblings so happy? They talked about difficulties when one had a relationship and the other didn't, including when one twin's boyfriend tried to involve the other twin in helping to solve the couple's problems. But they managed to get through such situations and claim that they look forward to future relationships, as long as each remembers not to be involved in the other's romantic problems.

What about friendships? In describing their social life, both sisters talked about enjoying casual friendships but not needing a close friend since their twinship more than satisfies that need. Victoria explained:

> We always introduce a friend to each other, and that person will auto-matically assume that they're friends of both of us. But I would never, ever expect a friendship to be as good as the relationship with my

twin. Because I know it can never be, and I don't expect it of a friend. It's like I don't really need it because I've got her. She's better than a friend. I don't really need someone who's a best friend because I have a best friend. So I wouldn't expect it to be an amazing friendship; I just expect it to be a friendship, and that's enough really.

Grace added:

We don't really have close best friends; we just have friends. We have different groups of friends, and we try to get our groups of friends to meet each other and be friends with each other. Victoria made a friend when she was on her own, and now that friend comes to visit us, so she's gotten to know me as well and is now my friend. And also the friend I made on my own got to know both of us. When our friends get to know the other one (of us), they're friends with the other one as well.

Like so much of the togetherness that exists between them, it seemed that both sisters earnestly approve of the social setup they've established— where a friend to one automatically becomes a friend to both. But during our conversation one twin would inject a slightly different perspective. For example, Victoria confessed it was nice to have her own friendship, apart from Grace:

But I like having a friend that doesn't know both of us because it can be more like they like me for who I am, instead of just meeting us as the twins. I have friends from when I was living here on my own. They know me more so they're more my friends. So I would go and see them without bringing her—just go and see them on my own, and just be more of a friend, an independent thing.

So it seems that one sister, at least, acknowledged the benefit of having a degree of independence, of being seen as an individual and experiencing life as separate from her twin.

And then there was the matter of arguments. It seems neither sister can tolerate the fact that they might have differing opinions about anything.

Somehow, this signifies to both that their twinship might be in jeopardy. When I asked Grace and Victoria what they tend to fight about, they brushed off the question at first, saying they argued about "really, really silly little things." But then they elaborated. First, Grace:

> A recent argument had to do with dinner. Victoria hadn't eaten as much as me, and I said, "What are you having for dinner?" and she said, "I can have whatever I want," and I said something like, "I know but you're hardly eating anything"—and then she got really annoyed that I commented on her dinner. So I'm not allowed to say anything about her dinner. And then I get annoyed that I can't have freedom of speech and say what I think. And then she gets mad. And this could go on for ages.

Victoria said:

> Or if she implied that she didn't want to do the job with me, then I would get really upset and then she would get annoyed that I was upset about that. It's like that: one of us is normally annoyed and the other one's upset.

Grace added:

> And then we get upset that the other one isn't comforting us, and then the one that's annoyed gets even more annoyed, or is crying because of something really silly. It is really silly, and then at the end we make up. And then we just say we're sorry, and then it's all fine.

I wondered if these arguments were, in fact, just silly or perhaps indicative of more serious, unacknowledged strains in the sisters' relationship. And was it really possible for everything to be smoothed over at the end of a fight, without an understanding of what the argument was fundamentally about? I suggested to Victoria and Grace that some of their arguments could be related to the fact that they seem to need to keep events and details so equal between them that when one veers off in a slightly different direction, their twin synchronicity feels disrupted, which then upsets them both. My explanation seemed to resonate, yet Grace reemphasized that the sisters feel more comfortable when they are on the same page:

> We have to make sure that our opinions are the same on the big issues. So if we're watching something on television, it can be really annoying if one of us makes a comment and the other one says, "No, I don't agree with that." We'll have a really big debate until we make sure we're basically on the same page.

I mentioned the fact that even spouses frequently disagree on various issues, and I asked the rhetorical question, "Why would two people—even though they are closely connected—always have to agree, given that they are two different people, with two different brains, and two distinct ways of thinking, evaluating, and feeling? If spouses feel entitled to their own point of view, why don't twins?" Victoria responded: "Yeah, that's how we would be with anyone else, but we're just not like that with each other. We just want the other person to think the same thing as us."

I then asked, "What would it feel like if you two had distinctly different opinions and ideas?"

"It would feel like we weren't as close," Victoria said.

Grace responded, "It would feel like we were just sisters."

"It's probably not really good that we're like that," Victoria confessed, "but we are."

Finally, we discussed the issue of secrets and privacy. It turns out that both sisters feel compelled to tell the other everything, in order to maintain their twin closeness, yet they both hinted that they desired the privacy they don't yet feel entitled to. Their statements reveal ambivalence about their self-imposed obligation to share all feelings and experiences with their twin. Victoria said:

> It can be really hard because sometimes you don't know how much to tell the other person. Like sometimes I feel that I should tell her everything, and then I have all these things I want to tell her, but I don't want to tell her everything. But I feel I have to.

Grace added:

> Sometimes I feel like I have to tell her something to make it okay. If
> I don't tell her, I don't know if it's okay or not. Like if I do something
> really embarrassing, I go to her and say, "Is it okay that I did that?"
> and she'll say, "Yeah, it's okay." And the fact that she says it's okay
> makes me feel much better about myself. It's like someone loves you
> no matter what.

When twins feel compelled to tell their sibling everything in an attempt
to maintain the strongest possible bond, it deprives both of privacy. Neither
person is entitled to keep his or her own feelings, ideas, or experiences
secret. Still, for overly close twins like Victoria and Grace, relinquishing
that privacy seems worthwhile because keeping secrets from the other
person results in tension and insecurity. Grace and Victoria rationalized
their lack of privacy by asserting that they did, in fact, have privacy from
other people—just not from each other. Although this distinction seemed
to be perfectly reasonable to them, their path toward discovering who they
are apart from one another will need to begin with the conviction that they
are entitled to their own private thoughts and experiences. Grace explained:

> It's like a normal person has privacy with themself, and we have
> privacy with us two. So we still have privacy from the outside world—
> we wouldn't tell everyone everything—but it's just between us that
> there's no privacy. But we have a lot of privacy and secrets from other
> people. So we tell each other secrets, and I know I can tell her some-
> thing and I know she won't tell anyone else. So in that way, it is like an
> extension of yourself.

Grace and Victoria have an enmeshed relationship. It is as if they want
and need to be one entity. Anything that disrupts their sense of identicality
is perceived as a threat, so that they cannot tolerate even minor disagreements because these disturb their collusive notion of being one person. Any
hint of differences, even the slightest crack in their façade of sameness (for
example, Grace's concern that Victoria isn't eating enough, which might

result in her weighing less than Grace) threatens the sense of security they both derive from being essentially one being.

How might these enmeshed twins become unstuck from each other? First of all, one of them would have to want that to happen. Perhaps when one sister becomes closely involved with a boyfriend and can no longer maintain the same degree of enmeshment with her sister, something will have to give. Or the crack in their wall of oneness might occur when one wants to have the freedom to maintain a friendship on her own, or quit the job they now share and do something else. At some point, one twin might seek therapy to explore whether living so closely in sync with a sibling is healthy.

Currently, however, Grace and Victoria seem to need to maintain a rigid degree of sameness and equality, thereby disallowing any meaningful self-reflection or development of distinct identities.

Connected and Independent—Hayley and Katherine

Hayley and Katherine were never as enmeshed as Victoria and Grace. They were, however, nearly inseparable growing up. The youngest of nine children, they depended on each other for the attention they rarely received from their single, working mother. Katherine explained what it was like:

> Our mom was married and divorced twice, and she didn't have a lot of money. She worked long hours, so she was never around—the older children raised the younger children. But Hayley and I were the youngest so we didn't get a lot of support. We acted as our own parents, and we gave each other unconditional love.

The sisters both talked about how they rooted for each other and provided each other with unconditional love that was never based on the need to be the same. In fact, Hayley said that individuality was always important to her, and she remembers feeling glad that her mother had not given her and Katherine matching names. Although the two accepted each other's distinct personalities and differences, there were times when their arguments were driven by a strong need to make the other see reality her way. Hayley remembers reaching a point when she could no longer tolerate fights that always seemed to result in bad feelings. So she made a decision to do things differently and tested her new strategy during what she referred to as "the sock incident":

> As teenagers, Katherine and I were always trying to argue our way out of a problem—screaming and yelling because she wasn't believing me and I wasn't believing her. We thought that was the end of the world, arguing like that. We would fight until we couldn't take it anymore, and we would exhaust ourselves. It was so important for us to agree on something that oftentimes it drove us apart.
>
> This one time I was about to put on a brand new pair of socks, but when I opened my drawer they weren't there. I went into Katherine's room, and I said, "Hey, did you take a pair of my socks?" and she said, "No"—and I knew she had. And so I just said, "Okay, well I really wanted to wear them tonight and I can't find them. But okay, thanks." Whereas, before I would have gone, "Don't tell me you didn't take them because I know you took them!" this time I took a different approach, went back into my room, and felt really good about giving her the space to come and bring the socks back to me. And it didn't take her but two minutes, and she was absolutely bawling: "I took your socks! I'm so sorry!"—and I let her off the hook as quick as I could, and I said, "Katherine, it's okay. It's alright. Don't worry about it. Thanks for returning them." And we felt closer after that.

When I asked Katherine how she and Hayley had learned to get along so well, forging a closeness that allowed for their individuality, she again mentioned the unconditional love between her and her sister. She also explained how the two had made an agreement when they were teenagers to treat each other with respect. She explained their pact in this way:

> We both attribute our success in life—and in our relationship—to the support and unconditional love that we've always had for each other. And there's something else: When we were about eighteen or nineteen we made a pact. We said we would treat each other like

friends, not family. Because sometimes with family there's a certain entitlement. And we just said, "We're gonna be kind and loving to each other"—so we knew whatever we said to the other person, the intention behind it was always supportive. It may not have been the best way to say it, but the overall intention came from a place of love and support. And that's how we've been able to grow.

When Katherine mentioned that the sisters wanted to avoid the behavior that some family members feel entitled to, I believe what she meant was feeling entitled to be overly judgmental or critical. And she and Hayley have tried very hard to avoid those behaviors. As they grew older, they didn't need the other to agree with them in order to feel close. Katherine said that after an argument, "we were always able to get the closeness back. Even if she went her way and I went my way, we were able to come together and feel the love."

After attending separate colleges, Katherine wanted to move to a different city but Hayley didn't because she did not want to leave her boyfriend. So Hayley begged Katherine to stay. Katherine agreed but made one significant stipulation. "I'll agree not to move," she said, "but you're going to owe me one." When Katherine met her future husband and moved to another state, she told Hayley, "I'm going to collect on that promise now," and Hayley made good on her payment, moving out of state with Katherine and her new husband. So each sister honored her firm commitment to live in the same town as the other; living apart did not seem feasible.

And then came the biggest shift in the sisters' relationship. When they were in their early thirties, Hayley made the decision to move across the country for an important career opportunity. But this time Katherine did not follow her. She knew it was a wonderful chance for Hayley to advance in her career, and she fully supported her sister's decision to relocate, but Katherine had a son and couldn't restructure their lives in order to follow her sister. Now divorced from her husband, Katherine's adjustment to being separated from Hayley wasn't easy.

Being on my own was absolutely the biggest change in my life. Hayley not being around was so hard for me. I have definitely, at times in my life, used Hayley as a crutch, like going to business events and being able to sit by her—rather than putting myself out there and mingling and introducing myself as an independent person. When Hayley left, I was already in business and running my own life, and a single mother and taking care of myself, so I was already doing some of those things; but without her, I was catapulted to a whole other level of independence and growth. I was out of my comfort zone, but I needed to be. It really helped me to grow into an individual person.

As for Hayley, although she is the one who instigated the move, separating from her twin wasn't easy for her, either.

We had leaned on each other, we always knew we had each other so it was very challenging for me to leave her and go someplace where I didn't have family. And she was more than family—it was the twin connection, where if anything ever happened to me, she would be right there. But I just figured it was going to be now or never for me.

Both sisters talked about how painful it was initially to be without the other. But each also spoke of how their separation provided the opportunity to learn more about themselves as individuals, and to test their ability to meet challenges on their own. The fact that each respected the other and continued to root for one another no matter what meant that Katherine would never have prevented Hayley from pursuing her dreams. And, as Hayley explained, Katherine never once made her feel guilty about the decision to move:

She never said, "Oh, you're leaving me. How can you do this?" She just said, "I understand. I'm upset, and I don't want you to go, but I understand." There was always that level of respect, of her acknowledging me as being an individual, without me having to feel guilty. She knew I wanted to go, and she was happy for me. I think it was one of the most courageous things for both of us to be able to handle my move with such grace.

Still, both women agree that they had to break through a great deal of fear when they first separated. Hayley spoke of them having been used to "leaning and relying on each other." And Katherine said she was "very, very afraid of being separated because we had never not been around each other our entire lives. So it was painful."

After Hayley's move, she and Katherine met for a series of seminars on love and fear, and each mentioned how the experience strengthened their belief in conquering their own fears of separation. Katherine commented:

> Hayley's move turned out to be a really wonderful gift and testament to our relationship. Because we're as close as ever and we make time for each other—on the phone, and I travel to see her and she travels to see me—but we've become independent from each other in terms of our own friendships, our own day-to-day lives. And that turned out to be a really good thing for our inner strength and personal development. It has been challenging and rewarding.

And Hayley added:

> Growing and learning with each other, we know how to take responsibility for our own emotions. We're twins, but we're also individual souls, and we have to support each other in making individual decisions. But we'll always have that sense that "You know I love you, and I'll always be there."

Assessing Your Feelings

The following are suggestions for further exploring your feelings about your twinship and how close you want your relationship to be.

- Try this exercise: Imagine that you are a singleton. Articulate your needs out loud, so that you can hear yourself speak. What feelings are triggered when you acknowledge what you want and feel? Do you feel guilty, afraid, awkward, ashamed? Be aware of those feelings.

- Ask yourself these questions, and reflect on what your answers reveal about your closeness to your twin:

▷ Am I concerned that I cannot be okay without my twin because I am too dependent upon her/him?

▷ Do I feel that I need my twin's presence to complete my sense of self?

▷ Do I wish my twin wasn't so dependent on me?

▷ Do I want to be able to share my true feelings with my twin, without worrying if she/he will feel hurt or take it the wrong way?

▷ Am I close to my twin because I feel obligated?

▷ Am I close to my twin because I need him/her?

▷ Am I close to my twin because I can be myself around him/her and enjoy his/her company?

Perhaps this is the first time you have considered these particular feelings in relation to your twin. It is quite possible that confronting your responses and facing the reality of your twinship will be unsettling. I would encourage you, however, to be honest with yourself and use this opportunity to think about how you would like your relationship with your twin to develop from this point forward.

Guidelines for Considering Your Twin Closeness

In the Adult Twin Survey at the end of chapter 1 are particular statements on the issue of twin closeness. Consider the following statements, which will help you assess your feelings about how close you are with your twin and whether or not you want to change that level of closeness:

- I feel hurt that my twin shuts me out of his/her life.

- I get very depressed when I think of how my twin and I have grown apart.

- I feel guilty for wishing that my twin lived somewhere else so that I could be more independent from her/him.

- I feel like I have to fake feeling closer to my twin than I actually feel.

- I hate it when my twin tells me how he/she wants us always to be as close as we were when we were kids. That's not how I feel.

- I'm envious of nontwins who enjoy a more normal relationship with their siblings.

3

My Twin, My Caretaker

*My sister is like a mother hen, but I usually just go along with her to
avoid a confrontation. When we do fight, I'm the one who gets nasty
because I am angry about being controlled.* —Adele, 31

*I take pride in my brother's accomplishments. I helped him get through
the army, gave him a start in our business. I had to nurse him along
because he was always so anxious and nervous.* —Gerard, 43

How does one twin become the "mother hen" and the other the "anxious"
follower who needs to be "nursed along"? Are twins destined for either
one role or the other? In my experience as a psychotherapist specializing
in twin issues, I have come to the conclusion that very often the caretaker dynamic takes over when parents of twins are not fully available
as parents. In such circumstances, one twin may become a parental-type
figure for the other.

Obviously, parents of twins have their hands full. What parent wouldn't
be frazzled trying to raise twins? Paying attention to two little ones at the
same time, attending to the needs of two same-age toddlers, kindergartners,
or eight-year-olds without losing your patience or your mind can seem
impossible. And when there are other siblings in the family as well, the

chaos and caretaking demands escalate. A common solution is to allow the twins to amuse or take care of each other. Since the twin mystique holds that twins are innately close companions and naturally look after one another, many parents believe that it makes perfect sense to leave same-age siblings in each other's care. Unfortunately, this arrangement can result in parents neglecting to be the authentic caregivers, mentors, and nurturers that every child needs. Given this parental vacuum, one twin assumes the role of caretaker and the other may come to depend on his or her sibling's caretaking. Some twins play these roles well into adulthood, with various repercussions.

Sometimes both siblings end up resenting each other; the caretaking twin resents having to be constantly responsible for his or her sibling, and the looked-after twin resents being constantly controlled. Neither has the freedom to lead her life as she chooses because the burden of either caretaking one's twin or waiting for a twin's guidance and approval always exists. Another familiar scenario is when one twin wants to continue the caretaker/cared-for relationship and the other doesn't. One twin may want to give up the role of either the controller or the controlled but doesn't want to abandon or hurt the other twin. And very often neither twin can be open about her needs and wants, so both must struggle with personal agendas that are at odds.

The twin caretaking dynamic doesn't always originate in families with parenting deficiencies, however. Most twin pairs consist of a more dominant sibling and a more accommodating one. Given that they are the same age, it is natural for one to take the lead and the other to follow. In some cases, one or both twins will remain in those roles throughout their childhood. In other cases, twins may take turns being the leader or the caretaker, depending on the particular situation.

A parent's interaction with the children is, of course, always a factor. For one thing, the compatibility between the parent's temperament and the child's is significant. Some parents might deal well with an easygoing child but have difficulty with an assertive one; others might have an easier time relating to a more assertive child and find it hard to relate to an accommodating one. So it makes sense that much of what happens in the parent-child relationship will be contingent on the fit between the child's personality and the parent's. This is a given with both singletons and multiples. With twins, the easygoing or assertive roles may be solidified depending on how the parent has interacted with both children.

Interestingly, the dominant/accommodating relationship can shift in adolescence or young adulthood so that twins switch roles, the dominant, caretaking twin becoming more dependent upon the other twin once that sibling becomes more independent.

In this chapter, we'll explore how the caretaking pattern takes hold in various ways and how hard it can be to break. And we'll hear from twins who have confronted this common issue.

Needing Your Twin versus Needing Your Space

Looking back at the Adult Twin Survey in chapter 1, it is interesting to note that certain statements are particularly relevant to the caretaking dynamic. If you put a checkmark next to to any of those statements, it might be an indication you are struggling with your role as either the caretaker or cared-for twin. However, there are no absolutes when it comes to twinships. Descriptions of what it feels like to be a caretaker or a cared-for twin vary according to the nature of your relationship and the circumstances you have faced throughout your lives. You may find that as the caretaker you still feel you need your twin to feel complete or that you've never had the chance to discover who you are apart from your twin. As the more needy or cared-for twin, you may long for more independence or wish that your caretaking twin would give you more emotional space.

As with other adult twinship issues, a caretaking continuum exists. At one end are those siblings who seem to be content with their caretaker/

cared-for relationship. At the other end are twinships where both twins want to break free from the caretaking dynamic. And somewhere in the middle are relationships where one twin is happy with the status quo but the other wants change. With these variations in mind, below are statements that reflect aspects of the caretaker/cared-for twinship.

Caretaker/Dominant Twin

Although the caretaking twin may feel burdened by his responsibilities, often he is reluctant to relinquish this role because it diminishes his sense of power and control.

- I don't know how to tell my twin I need more space without hurting her/his feelings.
- I can't concentrate on my own life because I'm constantly worried about my twin's well-being.
- I feel guilty for hoping my twin will replace me with someone else.

Cared-for/Dependent Twin

The cared-for twin lacks self-confidence and poise. Since he relies on his twin to feel comfortable and secure, he worries about being on his own.

- I feel ashamed of how much I still need my twin; I want to let go, but I'm terrified to be without his/her emotional support.
- I would be lost if my twin moved to another city.
- I've never had the chance to figure out who I am apart from my twin.

Why do some adults feel responsible for their twin's well-being? And why do others find it difficult to give up the attention and guidance they receive from their same-age sibling? Can twins care deeply for each other without assuming either the caretaker or cared-for role? In the stories that follow, adult twins from various backgrounds confront these core questions.

"I Became the Strong Twin She Could Depend On"— Tessa's Story

When Tessa and her twin sister, Keisha, were growing up, they enjoyed playing together and learning from each other. Since each girl was better at some activity than the other, the roles of leader and follower were somewhat interchangeable. Tessa offered the example that her sister was the one to take the lead when a hard-to-turn-on water faucet needed to be turned on, and Tessa was the one who took charge of money matters.

> When we were little, Keisha would hold out two quarters in her hand and ask me, "Do we have enough to buy candy?" She wouldn't even look at the coins; she'd just depend on me to figure it out. My parents told me she would turn to me often, so I guess you could say I was the strong twin.

It wasn't long before Tessa was called upon to become even stronger than she would have wished. When the girls were ten, Keisha became ill with a condition that took four years to diagnose. During that period, the family's focus was on attending to Keisha's needs, visiting a host of doctors, and getting to the bottom of Keisha's illness. Although Tessa doesn't recall her mother or father ever holding her to a particular code of behavior, she felt she had to withhold any feelings that might have further upset either her sister or her parents. But that didn't mean those feelings didn't exist.

> It was a really frustrating time for me because my parents never said it, but I was kind of expected to just be okay with how my sister's illness had changed our lives—because I didn't have the problems and she did. I became the strong twin she could depend on because I thought that's what my parents expected me to be. But I felt guilty for not feeling compassionate. My sister was sick and I was frustrated with her for having these problems. I came to resent her and really wished she didn't exist. I never talked about it to my parents. I think they would have been understanding if I had, but I didn't.

Tessa is now twenty-three. She started to cry when recalling the emotions that had overtaken her as a preteen. Being the strong twin had been a strain on her, but she felt guilty about admitting it—then and now. The burden of being her sister's emotional caretaker involved suppressing her own feelings and pretending she was fine. In fact, she said she hadn't thought about these issues for years and was surprised by her tears. I told Tessa that it was healthy for her to cry, that it must have been upsetting for her not to be able to say to her parents, "This is so unfair. I feel bad that Keisha is so sick, but she's getting all this attention, and I'm not getting any." Of course Tessa felt compassion for her sister, but she was also angry and frustrated. I explained to her that such emotions are normal when one sibling is ill and the healthy sibling feels she has to be perfect and well-behaved because the parents are overwhelmed by dealing with the sick child. Although Tessa's parents didn't stipulate that Tessa had to be the strong one, she felt the implicit need to be the dependable, caretaking twin sister she had always been.

Tessa made it clear that her parents were in no way to blame: she had taken it upon herself to respond as she had when she was younger. But it was apparent that her mixed emotions toward her sister—guilt, resentment, sadness, and compassion—were still with her.

> I think my parents would feel terrible if they knew how strongly I felt back then that I needed to be "perfect," but yeah, it was on me. Somewhere along the line I picked up the idea that I should be, for Keisha, as good as possible and not add anything more to the whole situation.

Tessa recalled one incident in particular when she thought about how her sister's illness had impacted her as a child. It may seem insignificant to an adult, but for eleven-year-old Tessa it signified the sacrifices she made in order to maintain her role as the caretaking strong one.

> My favorite food was macaroni and cheese. As a little kid, that was always my birthday meal. But due to my sister's condition, she was

put on various special diets, and to make things easier, my mom would only fix food that my sister could eat. If I were to eat something Keisha couldn't have, she'd get upset. My mom tried to explain that it would make my sister's sickness worse to eat those things. I remember one time crying myself to sleep because I was so frustrated that I couldn't have my favorite foods because my sister couldn't have them. And I think that was when I probably realized that I was resenting her.

Keisha's medical problems were finally resolved when the girls were in their early teens. Today, the sisters live in different cities. They are each completing their education and looking forward to careers. But when she's with her twin, Tessa still finds herself taking on the role of helpful guide, or as she puts it, "the solution person." And, according to Tessa, Keisha still seems to need that type of guidance. Whereas Tessa knows where she is headed professionally, Keisha is often self-doubting and unsure of which path to take. Tessa explained:

> I'm the one who will say, "Okay, this needs to be done," and I go and do it. Where she'll wait until somebody will do it with her, or will shove her and say, "You have to do it now." It'll happen where I've made a decision and finished something and she decided not to finish it, or it didn't look like she was going to do as well, so she'd be upset. She'd beat herself up and talk about "Why can't I ever complete anything or figure anything out" and just be in a real funk for a couple days. So I'm usually the one to try to make her feel better. In our twin-ship, I'm the solution person. I'll try to help her figure out, "Well, if you did this or this, you could complete it next year" or "You're on the right road" or whatever. I'll try to find the solution.

At twenty-three, Tessa has yet to become involved in a serious relation-ship and she said she has trouble making really close friends. She spoke of her ongoing closeness to her sister and how that has affected her ability to get close to others. One reason may be that being needed as "the solution person" and "the strong one" by her sister may have left Tessa feeling wary of other close relationships. Perhaps she believes that the kind of one-sided caretaking to which she has been accustomed is what relationships are all about. Or perhaps she needs someone to be there for her in the ways her sister never could be. Tessa confided that she is open to closer friendships and a serious relationship but is still learning how to connect with people in a deeper way.

> Keisha has always been my best friend. Up until her illness, we always did everything together. And then, in high school, after she got better, we started becoming better friends. But I've never had any friends that were closer than her. And I've had a hard time opening up to people that aren't my sister—to go from being just friends to being good friends. Explaining to someone that I'm hurting inside or upset about something—that's something that I wouldn't tell to just a regular friend. And I've had to learn to figure out which friends I can open up to and which friends are not people I can do that with.

Learning who you can trust and with whom you can be vulnerable is a challenge for anyone seeking a close relationship. For someone whose interpersonal experiences have essentially been limited to a twinship, those lessons can be particularly difficult. Tessa loves her sister and wants to stay connected to her, but she also knows the burden of being a caretaker. At this point in her life, she would like to find out who she is beyond the caretaking twin she has always been.

> I have struggled with the bond and dependencies of being a twin. I've had to work hard to know that I am me, and that what she does or doesn't do, isn't me. I'm still figuring out what coming into a close relationship means, and who I am individually.

"I Don't Want to Be Controlled by Her Anymore"—Adele's Story

Needing your twin and at the same time wanting your independence from her is a dilemma that many twins confront. For the cared-for twin, being mothered by your same-age sibling may feel like a familiar necessity, but there comes a point when the caretaking dynamic becomes oppressive.

Such was the case with Adele. Now in her early thirties, Adele recently moved across the country to get away from her sister. "We're close, but we fight a lot," she explained.

Adele and her twin sister, Alexandra, went to the same college and lived together as roommates. The pattern they had established in childhood largely persisted during their college years, with Adele accommodating to Alexandra's plans and decisions. At the same time, Adele made it a point to choose a different major than her sister so she could begin charting a separate course. And although Adele continued being the easygoing twin who tended to accede to her twin sister's wishes, a noticeable shift in their twinship occurred. In their last few years of college, Adele began to rebel against her sister's hold over her by verbally lashing out. Adele explained:

> My sister is like a mother hen, but I usually just go along with her to avoid a confrontation. When we do fight, I'm the one who gets nasty because I am angry about being controlled.

The push-pull of sometimes following her sister's lead and other times striking out on her own was evidenced after Adele graduated college. She and Alexandra both worked for the same company for a while and joined the same sports club, but Adele spent several nights a week taking specialized classes that would lead to a better position in her field. Eventually she was able to land a job in a new city, thousands of miles from her sister. Proud of herself for following her own path and making the move, Adele nonetheless missed Alexandra. It wasn't always easy adjusting to a life without her constant companion of twenty-plus years, her lifelong caretaking twin.

Before long Adele was involved with a man who filled the space left by her sister. They began their relationship as best friends, and unlike other men she had dated, this person really wanted to get to know her. The couple enjoyed long walks and in-depth conversations, which Adele appreciated and valued. The boyfriend seemed to be loving and respectful, and Adele found herself falling in love with him. But ultimately the romance deteriorated. Adele commented on certain elements in this relationship that resembled her twinship with Alexandra:

> We were so close, and at first it seemed we could talk about anything. We were best friends. But I started to notice that I was constantly compromising myself in order to please him. He demanded that I see things his way, insisting that I change my views on things that really mattered to me, and I just couldn't do it.

Adele broke up with her boyfriend when he became too demanding. He was paternalistic and controlling and unable to accept her as she is. Given that it had taken her so long to begin to become her own person, someone separate from her sister, she wouldn't allow herself to be controlled by someone else. Her twinship experience had contributed to her attraction to this man; he could fill the caretaker role she had given up when she moved away from her sister. But her relationship with Alexandra had also taught her to walk away from a situation where she would have to sacrifice who she was in order to be loved.

Adele and Alexandra are still in close touch. Through phone calls and e-mails they tell each other what's going on in their separate lives. Adele said that each had also shared something recently that neither would have expected the other to say years ago: they like living apart. "It's a relief," Adele said, "not to be so dependent on each other."

How the Twin Caretaking Dynamic Can Affect One's Choice of Partners

Twins who have experienced the caretaker dynamic may consciously or unconsciously choose partners who fill the same or opposite roles as their same-age sibling. For instance, like Adele, cared-for twins may be attracted to someone who will assume the caretaker role. Such a relationship may or may not work out, depending on the individuals involved. In Adele's case, her boyfriend was overly controlling and would have prevented her from developing as an individual. After a lifetime of being controlled by her caretaking sister, Adele was wise enough to cut off the relationship before she was in too deep. In other instances, however, the caretaking partner may allow the twin more space, providing enough nurturance to make the twin feel comfortable but avoiding any oppressive, controlling behavior.

On the other hand, a twin whose sister or brother was the caretaker may be attracted to a partner who is far less dominant and intrusive than her or his twin. Such an attraction may be based on the prospect of being more of an equal with one's lover or spouse, thereby allowing a previously cared-for twin to freely develop her or his independence and sense of self.

As for the caregiver twin who has never been on the receiving end of emotional support or guidance within the twinship, he or she may be drawn to a caregiver partner—someone who will provide those benefits. Weary of the dominant twin role, such individuals may welcome someone who will be willing to take charge and be the nurturer. Or, a caregiver may choose another person with whom she can continue her role as nurturer and guide because giving up that position can be traumatic. Without someone to look after, a caretaker twin is faced with turning her attention to herself, which is not always easy to do.

"No Matter How Much I Take Care of Her, She Still Feels I'm Not There for Her"—Beatrice's Story

Beatrice is forty-two and married with three children. She summarized her present circumstances as follows: "I have a full-time job, I have a mortgage, and I have my twin sister, who is bipolar." Beatrice's sister, Daisy, has been in and out of institutions, is unable to hold a job, and has lived with Beatrice off and on over the last twenty years. To say that Daisy is dependent on Beatrice is an understatement. Beatrice feels so overwhelmed that she doesn't know how she can continue to hold together all the stressful pieces of her life. The greatest stressor seems to be her commitment to her twin, which she described in the following way:

She is so needy. She's coming out of another breakdown now and feels
like I'm not there for her. I don't know how to say it in any other way:
I am her rock. And yet, it's like having a fourth child.

The girls were raised by their maternal grandparents after their biological parents were killed in a car accident when the girls were four years old.
According to Beatrice,

A codependency, if you will, developed. I think that was pretty
unhealthy because we had nobody else really. But had we not had
each other . . .

Beatrice and Daisy had each other for a number of years but were
separated at age eleven. "Our grandparents decided that we needed
to become individuals," Beatrice said, implying with sarcasm that her
relatives had been less than sensitive in depriving the sisters of the
only emotional anchor they had. The girls had little contact with each
other after that point. Beatrice finished high school; Daisy dropped out.
Beatrice attended college, married, and had a child; Daisy got caught
up in drugs and the rave scene. Beatrice believes that Daisy's bipolar
condition developed in her late teens around the time Daisy started
taking a lot of drugs.

Beatrice didn't approve of Daisy's lifestyle and was trying to carve out
a stable life for herself. Then, when they were twenty-one, Daisy tried to
commit suicide. Beatrice immediately went to her:

I came out to be with her for that, and it was significant for me
because at that point I felt deeply betrayed; I felt like she had chosen
to leave the planet and leave me here by myself. In terms of the twinship, it was a total betrayal of our twinship. Now I understand that was
the beginning of her bipolar illness, but they hadn't diagnosed her yet.

Several years later, Daisy was hospitalized for a drug- and alcohol-
induced psychotic breakdown. After being released, Daisy began living
with Beatrice and her family. She has been "in and out of breakdowns

ever since," according to Beatrice, and Daisy sometimes feels the need to be with Beatrice every second. "I literally couldn't go to the bathroom," Beatrice said. "I was the only one who made her feel safe." But Beatrice isn't the only one impacted by Daisy's condition. It recently had a devastating effect on Beatrice's oldest daughter, who believed she was also hearing voices and hallucinating, just like her Aunt Daisy. As if overseeing Daisy wasn't stressful enough, Beatrice also had to cope with the friends and lovers Daisy brought home. At one point she had a boyfriend who was violent and threatened to kill her.

It was then that Beatrice realized she couldn't take care of Daisy in her home anymore; not only was she at her wit's end, but Beatrice refused to put her children at risk any longer. Daisy presently lives down the street from Beatrice, and because she has no other way to earn a living, Beatrice has hired her part-time at the company she manages. So Daisy is still closely connected to Beatrice, and the demands placed on Beatrice by her sister's illness and neediness have taken a toll on Beatrice's marriage as well. She and her husband are in therapy trying to work out some issues, but their relationship is in trouble.

With all of these issues to deal with, Beatrice continues to feel an obligation to Daisy because they're sisters—and because they're twins. She explained it this way:

> It is so beyond just a regular sibling. My friends say to me, when Daisy is having a breakdown, "What are you doing trying to take care of her?" I can't quite explain it, but when she's having a psychotic breakdown, it is truly devastating for me, and to have to feel her terror and then guide her back to sanity—not that the doctors aren't doing it and the meds aren't doing it—but for me it is soul-shattering. And it's a responsibility. But it is these difficulties in my twinship that I endure. And the worst part is, she told me the other day she feels like I'm not there for her. Even though my husband and I are in the middle of one of the biggest crises of my own life, the fact that she says to me, "You're not there for me," I feel like I'm failing.

Even a "regular" sibling would feel torn by the wrenching circumstances Beatrice currently faces. How could anyone stand by and do nothing when a family member is having such a hard time? When such suffering involves a twin, the stakes can seem even higher and the required sacrifice more essential. As Beatrice put it, Daisy's terror and her need to be guided back to sanity become "soul-shattering" for Beatrice. But as I explained to her, there is a point at which one has to care for one's own well-being at least as much as one cares for a loved one—otherwise, the sacrifice is too great. I told Beatrice, "For the last twenty years you have been there for your sister when she needed you, helped her cope with dangerous and unhealthy situations even when circumstances put your own family at risk. It is clear that you feel a deep connection with her. But you cannot allow your sense of responsibility as her twin to undermine your own health, your children's safety, and your marriage."

Beatrice said she felt guilty for being angry at her sister for needing her so much. I assured her that her response is normal. Twins often feel they don't have the right to be angry about their twin's demands. This is because it is assumed that twins will always need each other and should take care of each other no matter what. But I told Beatrice that she had every right to feel aggravated and annoyed. It is clear that Daisy is in no shape to be able to appreciate what Beatrice does for her, which is why she continues to demand more and more. Rather than feeling as if she has failed when Daisy tells her, "you aren't there for me," Beatrice needs to put into perspective how much she has already sacrificed.

Beatrice cannot save her sister; Daisy's addiction and mental illness are problems that require professional help. But Beatrice can work toward saving her own marriage by giving it the attention it deserves. It won't be easy for Beatrice to let go of the need to be Daisy's caretaker because it has been a role she has played for more than half her life. Putting herself and her family ahead of her twin sister will be a major change; nonetheless, Beatrice realizes she must rearrange her priorities if she is to nurture her marriage, protect her children, and have her own life. She will need to set boundaries with her sister and be more assertive with her regarding what she is willing and able to do to help her. And she will need to learn not to worry about her sister being dissatisfied with the level of help Beatrice is prepared to give.

I told Beatrice that every time she starts to feel guilty for not doing enough for her sister, she should keep in mind that her family's well-being is at stake. "I agree," Beatrice said, "my heart can only be so heavy. I have to sustain my own life. I can't carry all that."

"I Want to Find My Own Competency without Being Under His Control"—Anthony's Story

The way his twin brother, Gerard, views their personal history, Anthony owes whatever success he has achieved to Gerard. Gerard claims he helped Anthony get through the army, start a business, and cope with emotional ups and downs. Anthony acknowledges that Gerard is the take-charge twin, but after a lifetime of being in his brother's shadow Anthony is determined to find his own way.

Anthony and Gerard were born to parents who believed in the twin mystique. The boys were assumed to share a special unbreakable bond, and because they were twins their every milestone and effort was cause for comparison. The two were constantly measured against one another, whether it was how fast they swam, how many As they got, or how popular they were in school. It seems that Anthony never matched up, either in his own eyes or his family's. "My whole life I was second-rate and second best," he said. "It was just the way I was viewed and perceived by everyone, including me." Gerard's dominance over his submissive twin was assumed to be the natural order of events, and Anthony believed it was his role to follow behind his brother.

Gerard's inflated sense of entitlement was driven by the fact that he was favored by his mother and viewed as the stand-in father when the boys' father left the family in their early teens. Unfortunately, Gerard's caretaking of Anthony took the form of emotional abuse and control. Gerard insisted that his leadership decisions and powers were unquestionably legitimate, and that Anthony was completely incapable of managing his own life. He infantilized his twin brother, leading Anthony to believe that he couldn't do anything without Gerard's guidance and approval.

After they finished college, Gerard started a business and included Anthony in the company. According to Gerard, he went above and beyond to help his brother, who didn't have the fortitude required to launch a new venture. "Anthony had a job in retail and was going nowhere," Gerard said, "so I asked him to join my company and I had to nurse him along. He was always so anxious and nervous that the company wouldn't take off." Meanwhile, Anthony shared with me that Gerard constantly reminded him that he should be grateful to him, because if it weren't for Gerard, Anthony would be nowhere; he wouldn't have a business and he wouldn't have a life.

But Anthony did get a life. He married, has two young children, and is very involved with his family. As might be expected given his relationship with Gerard, Anthony chose a spouse who is the dominant one in their marriage. They both want to work on changing that dynamic, however, so that they can become more equal in the relationship. At this point, Anthony often looks to his wife, Candice, for direction—sometimes without being aware of it. Candice says he will often mirror her; for instance, she will make a comment and then a few days later Anthony will say the same thing and act as if he is stating it for the first time, as if it is his idea. She also complains that Anthony has difficulty being assertive. Still, Candice understands why it is hard for Anthony to be his own person and is supportive of his desire to break free of his controlling brother. Candice has little patience for her brother-in-law's hurtful condescension toward Anthony and resents Gerard saying comments like "Anthony has come a long way since I first took him under my wing" and "I take pride in Anthony's professional growth." Gerard's narcissistic, paternalistic perspective undermines the progress Anthony has made due to his own efforts and talents. On the other hand, when the business began to fail due to Gerard's miscalculations and ineffective leadership, Gerard blamed everyone but himself. According to Anthony, Gerard brought down the business:

> Without consulting me, Gerard made very unwise business decisions that made no sense to anyone else in the firm. Now that I have a better perspective on my dealings with him over the years, I realize that he has screwed up pretty much everything he has been involved in. If he hadn't been my brother, I would never have continued to be in business with someone who makes such stupid decisions and lacks basic interpersonal skills.

The business eventually folded, which became a positive turning point for Anthony. It forced him to more clearly assess his brother's controlling behavior—and to realize how it had adversely affected him since childhood. Candice reinforced Anthony's new perspective. She brought to his attention that he need not continue seeing himself as second best or unable to be his own person, as Gerard had brainwashed him into feeling throughout their lives. Anthony finally feels free to become the man he believes himself to be—an individual with talents and skills, a loving family, and the ability to shape his own life. He admits that it is still hard for him to stand up to Gerard, but he is determined to follow through with his commitment to himself. "I am sick of this," he said. "I need my own experience, my own identity, my own manhood."

The caretaking twin often suffers the most when his or her twin finally breaks away. With no one to oversee, or in Gerard's case to control, the caretaker often experiences a loss of identity. He is forced to question who he is and what his role should be once he no longer is responsible for someone else. It is almost like the empty nest syndrome, when parents whose lives have largely been defined by their parenting roles must face a kind of existential dilemma. For the dominant caretaking twin, it can be very difficult to shift into a life more focused on oneself than on one's sibling.

"My Sister Was the Maternal Twin, and I Was the Carefree One!"—Pamela's Story

An interesting aspect of the twin caretaking dynamic is that sometimes the cared-for twin can grow up to feel far less burdened by her childhood role than the caretaker sibling. Such is the case with Pamela and her twin sister, Linda, who are now in their early fifties.

I interviewed the two separately. One of the first memories Pamela shared was she hated that she and her sister were "lumped together as a unit" when they were children. She took it for granted, though, that Linda was like a mother to her. In fact, the girls' mother was mentally unstable and never very available to either of them, so Linda's mothering of Pamela was a necessity.

After a brief stint in college, Pamela lived on her own for a while, which she found challenging and difficult. The sisters would talk to each other every day—sometimes twice a day—and still do. When Linda got married, Pamela figured that she should also get married, which she did several years later. Pamela's husband later pointed out to her that she had a pattern of doing whatever Linda did without really thinking about it. Another example of this was after Linda had a baby, Pamela had one eighteen months later. It seems it was natural for Pamela to follow in Linda's footsteps.

Although both Pamela and Linda have careers, Pamela feels that her life has been more carefree than her sister's and worries that perhaps Linda resents her for this. She put it this way:

> I think I have had more fun in my life than Linda because I'm more of a free spirit. Linda has always been in the maternal role, not only with me but with our parents, too. When they were sick, she was the one who would rush over there and take care of them. She probably resents me for not taking on as much of the responsibility.

Pamela says she feels guilty that Linda has had to assume the lion's share of caregiving in their family. "But mostly I feel sad for her," she said.

Linda is used to her maternal role. She remembers as a child being hypervigilant with respect to her twin sister's needs. While she referred to her role as a burden, Linda also credits it with having made her stronger than Pamela. This is how she described her early caretaking role:

> I was always the caretaker, bearing the burden of my third roving eye that kept watch over my sister. Our family photos show one worried, unsmiling twin while the other is happy, carefree, and smiling. But I think I've developed a resilience and strength that Pamela did not have to develop because I was the caretaker.

After looking after her sister for years, Linda became not only strong and resilient but responsible, dependable, and caring toward everyone with whom she comes in contact. At work, Linda says she has difficulty delegating responsibility and is overly worried about everyone's well-being. She admits she would rather focus on other people than on herself, and added, "I am terrific at being another person's advocate." Unfortunately, the flip side of her caretaking role is that Linda feels uncomfortable when people attempt to reciprocate her kindness; she worries that they are going out of their way or being burdened on her behalf. She explained that when she and Pamela were in their midthirties, their caretaking roles shifted during the time she (Linda) was going through a divorce from her first husband. "I loved the fact that Pamela was taking care of me then," Linda said, "but I felt guilty because I thought I should be able to stand on my own two feet."

Linda's sense that she is not entitled to the same sisterly nurturing and attention she had always given Pamela attests to how steadfastly she has clung to her caretaker role. Linda feels uncomfortable receiving emotional support. The fact that neither sister had been adequately nurtured by her mother is key to Linda's reaction to being cared for now. Although Pamela received nurturing from Linda when they were children, nobody ever offered nurturing to Linda, so she neither received it nor expected it.

Consequently, when people want to take care of her, Linda feels unentitled and often rejects their efforts.

A recent disagreement between the sisters became an important turning point for both. They had an argument about Linda's husband, and Pamela got angry with Linda for putting up with his behavior. Linda screamed at Pamela, telling her to get out of her house. After the fight, they did not speak for months. The sisters had never before had a screaming fight; they had always been able to work through their disagreements.

Pamela finally called Linda and apologized, telling her that she had had no right to criticize Linda's husband. Pamela took responsibility for her actions and for the rift between them. Linda forgave her. It was a relatively minor squabble, but no family feud is minor when it means two people stop speaking to each other. The incident was particularly significant for these adult twin sisters in that Pamela confessed something she had never fully realized before. "I felt that my twinship gave me the right to say whatever I wanted, and that is not right," she said. Since Linda had always been her loving caretaker, Pamela felt that no matter how she behaved she would always be loved and accepted by Linda. The fact that Linda drew the line with Pamela by telling her to leave her home established a boundary between acceptable and unacceptable behavior. In that instance, by standing up for herself Linda demonstrated that she was taking care of herself, instead of her twin sister. And Pamela got it.

Linda said that since that conflict, the sisters' relationship feels more grown up, "like two adults, not a parent/child relationship."

Caring versus Care-Taking

The stories in this chapter highlight some of the issues adult twins face when the caretaking dynamic defines their relationship. Unlike the roles of parent and child, which gradually change as the child develops and becomes increasingly autonomous, very often twins do not change their relationship to one another. So the roles of caretaker and cared-for twin continue into adulthood. One of the reasons this fixed scenario exists is that according to our culture a twinship is not supposed to change; the twin mystique dictates that same-age siblings should be dependent on each other forever. The other reason is that the role one plays in another's life can be very difficult to give up. When a person is used to being emotionally taken care of by someone he or she loves, it can be a struggle to become more independent. And it can be equally painful for the caretaker, who may feel a great loss when the other twin pulls away. But self-reliance is essential to becoming one's own person.

There is a difference between caring about someone and taking care of that person. Caring about your twin involves sharing in your brother's (or sister's) joys and hardships and being there when you are needed for emotional support. It doesn't mean guiding or controlling your twin's life or sacrificing your own life for his. When you care about your twin, you allow him to become who he wants to be, on his own terms and in his own way. And loving your twin then becomes more authentic and more meaningful. You love him for who he is, not because he needs you.

Guidelines for Dealing with the Twin Caretaking Dynamic

Given that the caretaking pattern is often established in childhood, confronting it can be challenging. The key is to begin reflecting on these questions:

- How did your role in the twinship become defined in your childhood?

- How do you feel now as the caretaker or cared-for twin?

- How have your other relationships been affected by the caretaking dynamic that exists between you and your twin?

- What do you think might happen if you abandon your caretaking or cared-for role?

- What steps could you take to give up either role?

4

Separation Blues

My brother had to leave the country for three months, and I was lost and lonely. I became more productive because I'm lazy when he's around. There's nothing I'd rather do than just be with him, but without him I know I would be more focused on my own life. I could change this situation if I wanted to but I don't want to because I love him so much. —Victor, 33

My twin moved away six years ago, and it was devastating. But it was also one of the best things that ever happened to me because I became my own individual. We had a business together, and I depended so much on her for everything. She was always wanting to be in charge, and I was like, "Okay, okay we'll do it your way." Her moving away helped me realize that I can do things on my own. —Gail, 37

Adult twins often struggle with the decision to finally separate their life from their twin's. Once they make that decision, or once it is made for them, navigating life without their twin as a constant companion can be a challenge as well. Although separation in this sense doesn't imply not seeing one another or not being close friends, it does mean getting divorced from the "twin marriage." It involves making your own decisions, focusing on your own needs and goals, and living your life as an individual rather than as half of a pair. Many twins feel a profound ambivalence about living a separate life. Their head may tell them one thing but their heart pulls in another direction. Their relief at no longer being entwined with their sibling and finally having the chance to discover who they are as an individual is offset by intense feelings of insecurity, anxiety, sadness, or guilt.

Like Gail, some twins don't begin to find themselves until one twin physically moves away. Putting physical distance between the two of you can certainly jump-start the process of individuating, but it is not necessary. What is crucial is the desire to have the same freedoms and opportunities as a singleton and to become who you want to be without relying on or feeling responsible for your same-age sibling. In this chapter we'll hear from adult twins who are at various stages in the process of separation, including Luke, a college student who is living apart from his twin and making progress toward becoming his own person; Gail, who is delighted to have her own business but still misses the daily contact with her sister; Victor, who is still ambivalent about focusing on his own life; and Nancy, who had an epiphany at twenty-eight and told her parents, "I don't want my twin sister to be my only close relationship!"

As Gail mentioned, separating from one's twin can be a devastating process because giving up the ultraclose ties to someone you love more than anyone in the world—even if those ties are holding you back—is not easy, nor is relinquishing a lifestyle that feels secure and familiar. But just as a high school graduate leaves the nest to make his or her way in the world, a time comes in every twin's life when leaving the security of a twin-centered life is necessary in order to make one's way as a fully individuated adult.

In developmental psychology, *individuation* refers to the process by which a person becomes his or her true self. This process involves the integration over time of one's innate personality and one's life experiences. But a person cannot fully engage in the individuation process if his or her personality or life experiences are being regulated by the demands of an overly close twinship. You cannot find yourself if you are stuck in a relationship, however loving and secure it may seem, where you are prevented from discovering who you are. Sacrificing security in order to develop and grow is an ongoing theme in most people's lives. For twins, it often means feeling the temporary discomfort of living more independently from your same-age sibling. This was the case with Luke, who is now twenty-one but separated from his twin when they went to different colleges several years ago.

"When I Went Away to College, It Felt Like I Had Lost My Super Powers"—Luke's Story

Luke and his twin brother, Charlie, were raised in what Luke described as a "reserved" yet "very close-knit" family. Although Charlie was born only a few minutes before Luke, Charlie's father told him, "You are the oldest, so that's your role." Striving to be better than his older brother, Luke felt a sense of healthy competition as they were growing up. He explained:

> I always felt compelled to compete with Charlie in everything. I wanted to be better than him, and I was competitive in academics, sports, girls—even though we were terrible with girls. When we got our grades back, I remember comparing math scores. I'd ask, "What'd you get?" and he'd say, "ninety-four, what did you get?" and I'd go, "Ah, ninety-two!"

Charlie may have gotten higher math scores, but Luke was the more outgoing, sociable twin, and throughout their school years he took full advantage of the twin celebrity factor. He figured, perhaps unconsciously at first, that as long as he was receiving so much attention for being a twin, he would use it to his benefit by getting to know people and honing his social skills. Unfortunately, this method of connecting with people backfired when Luke entered college and no longer had Charlie around. He told me,

> A lot more people pay attention to you when you're a twin, so growing up I dealt with being the center of attention. There are two ways you can react: negatively, like "What are you staring at?" or

positively, and use it as an opportunity to meet new people. You can grow from these experiences of people just being interested in who you are because you look exactly like someone else. Receiving all that extra attention, I thrived off of that personal interaction and it made me develop an attractive personality. I don't want to blow myself up and say, "I'm the greatest," but I can sit down with someone, and they can tell I'm genuinely interested in what they have to bring to our relationship.

But when I first got to college, I found it really hard to relate to anyone. I struggled; I don't know why. I just wish I'd had some way of addressing that. Like if someone had just told me, "It is going to be hard to separate from your twin—at any stage of your life." Probably the longer you wait, the more difficult it gets.

Making casual friends wasn't the only challenge Luke faced once at college. He told me that not seeing his brother every day was really hard at first. He realized that he had taken their relationship for granted and that without Charlie he was a different person. "It felt like I had lost my super powers," he said. "No longer was I able to be in two places at once, or share thoughts with my best friend face-to-face." Luke had always looked to Charlie as a confidant; if he had a problem or something he wanted to discuss, Charlie was the first person he'd go to. Now there was no one to fill that role. It wasn't that Luke didn't have friends on campus; he did. But separating from Charlie meant he had to learn how to open up to others who had the potential of becoming close friends. As is the case with many twins, Luke was so used to having his brother understand him without Luke having to explain himself, that figuring out how to connect with a new person on a deeper level was daunting. Luke put it this way:

It is still hard for me to open up. It takes me a long time to tell anyone how I am feeling because I'm not used to talking about how I feel. I'm accustomed to Charlie just knowing without my having to put it into words. I didn't have to tell him, "Look, man, I'm going through some-thing" because he already recognized it. So he could just say, "Hey, man, I know it's this, this, and this. What are you gonna do about it?"

Whereas, in college no one knew if I was going through something or not. And I'm not going to just hang out with someone once or twice and then tell them my life story.

Luke is learning that he needs to spend enough time with someone in order to develop the trust that will allow him to feel comfortable opening up. And he recognizes that a new friend cannot be expected to understand him in the same way his twin does. Luke wants to make the separation from his brother work to his benefit. He wants to use this time in college to develop as an individual and discover aspects of himself he may not have had a chance to develop when he functioned more as a twin. For example, he spoke about wanting to compete with himself now, rather than with Charlie:

> I had to learn how to be motivated without the competition I always had with my brother. When I went off to school it was hard to find that motivation apart from Charlie. Now, I'm going to school for me, it is not like a competition. Whereas before it was "Must beat Charlie!" now it's "Must better myself!" I finally figured it out. I wish I'd figured it out sooner.

And speaking of figuring it out, Luke talked about how well Charlie is getting along socially without him. Although Luke was always the one to make new friends, Charlie is now handling that easily:

> In high school, Charlie just wasn't as prone to stepping into the lime-light. He liked watching me do things, and then he'd feed off of that or jump into it. But he wouldn't be the one to initiate it. But when he went to college, he thrived. When I visited him, he had made tons of friends and was doing just fine over there. He's so cool—I'm so proud he's my brother.

Both Charlie and Luke are making the adjustment to leading separate lives, and it is working out beautifully for them. They still value their close relationship and look forward to spending time together; but, as Luke put it, they are both "thriving" apart. Luke had to initially confront the loneliness and insecurity of being on his own. He had to develop new social skills to compensate for the loss of his twin celebrity status. And he had to learn how to become a self-motivator, rather than a twin competitor. Now that he has some perspective on the changes he's been through in the last several years, he appreciates the inner work he did to separate from his brother. When I asked him what he would have wanted in a book about adult twins, had he been able to pick one up on his way to college, he said:

> If I had been able to read something that addressed the separation issues, that would have been awesome. If I could have known, yeah, it's hard but then it gets better . . . and you can grow confident in your-self, aside from your twin.

"I Realized I Can Do Things on My Own"—Gail's Story

Growing up in an abusive family, Gail and her twin sister, Fran, were forced to adapt to a violent environment. Unfortunately, this resulted in their treating each other abusively. But as Gail explained, she and Fran were also each other's best friend:

> All we knew was violence. So we were extremely violent toward each other. We didn't know any better. The only way to solve a problem, the only thing we knew, was to beat or hit . . . so the fighting, yes, but we were also best, best friends. Until this day, at thirty-seven, we have issues when we're together for too long a time. Like, I love her with all my heart—we talk twenty thousand times a day—but even the last time she was here to visit me, it almost ended in a devastating way.

The sisters depended on each other when they were young, but Gail said she was more dependent on Fran, who took a greater leadership role. After high school, the two opened a small boutique together. Again, Fran tended to be in charge. "If a phone call had to be made or a crisis had to be attended to," Gail said, "she'd be the one to do it. She just had more confidence than I did."

According to Gail, Fran also had a need to be at the center of Gail's life, no matter what. Gail got married before Fran, and at Gail's rehearsal dinner Fran gave a self-centered speech that included how upset she was about losing her sister. Given their overly close relationship, Fran's reaction to Gail's marriage seemed tinged with the sort of anxiety and jealousy that is particularly evident in certain twinships. Gail explained:

> When I got engaged, Fran was horrific to me. It was the nightmare of my whole life; that whole year of planning my wedding she was the devil from hell with me. And her speech at my rehearsal dinner was so embarrassing—it was all about her and how it traumatized her when I got engaged. Nobody could believe what she was saying. People were like, "What the hell was that?" I remember thinking, "Is this really happening?" I thought she would be happy for me!

When Gail and I talked about why Fran had been so hurt by Gail's marriage, Gail referred to the fact that their twinship had been like a marriage and that Fran had felt as if they were now getting a divorce. Gail explained:

> I think Fran just felt . . . it was like we had this marriage for so long. She and I were the two that were together, and I think she thought this meant it was like a divorce. I would be leaving her to be with my husband, and I think she was mad at me for that. Maybe not knowing it, but she was angry. Or maybe she thought, "Gail is marrying this man and now I'm not the number one person in her life." And so I think she was hurt and blaming me, not really knowing she should not have been.

A year and a half later, Fran got married—and she got pregnant before Gail. It turns out that Gail had a similar reaction when Fran announced she was going to have a baby. She told me that she thought to herself, "Oh my God. My sister's pregnant and I'm not going to be the number one person in her life anymore." In other words, they were each still vying for the primary position in the other's life, tied to each other in an unhealthy way. Although they were adults with families of their own, neither seemed to be able to define herself as separate from the other.

Meanwhile, their business flourished, in part due to their twinship. Customers flocked to their boutique not only to buy the trendy fashions but to see the beautiful twin sisters who ran the shop. Then Fran's husband got a job offer in another state and Fran had the opportunity to open a store there. So they moved. Gail was initially "devastated," a word she used a lot when referring to how she has often reacted to Fran's overbearing behavior. But the separation enabled Gail to grow as both a person and as a businesswoman as she noted in the following comments:

> Fran moving away was so devastating to me, but it was also one of the best things that ever happened to me because I became my own individual. I had depended so much on her for everything, and I kind of fell behind her because she was always wanting to be in charge, and I was like "Okay, okay we'll do it your way." Where now, I have my own individual style in terms of what I buy for the store and how the store looks—and I am my own person. Her moving away helped me realize that I can do things on my own.

Gail's realization did not happen overnight. She was initially angry at Fran and her husband for following through with their plan to move. She was also terribly anxious and fearful. She was afraid she wouldn't be able to handle the store on her own, and that customers would no longer be attracted to the boutique because its unique "twin owners appeal" was gone. But without Fran as the mover and shaker, Gail had the opportunity to finally do what she wanted to do. She no longer had to accommodate Fran's wishes. Rather than remain stuck in the secondary role she had played since childhood, Gail could take charge of the store—and her own life. When asked how long it took to adjust to Fran's absence, Gail explained:

> I think it took me about a year. I missed her every day, and I was angry at her husband for taking her away. I was scared to death to run the store by myself. I was scared that nobody was going to like me for

me, that nobody would like me without my sister. Who was I without her? It was scary for me to not be special anymore. Who was going to come to the shop if it was just me? It wouldn't be like having the experience of "the twins." So I thought, "What am I going to give back to get that respect that we had as twins?" And it didn't hit me until I realized that my customers loved the few changes I'd made in the store. Yes, they missed Fran, but they still came. I established myself as the owner, Gail—not Gail and Fran, the twins who owned that cool boutique. So it took me a year before I was solidly on my feet, knowing "Okay, I can do this on my own."

Gail is proud of her own progress. She feels more grounded in terms of who she is as an individual and now knows she can achieve success and realize goals without her sister's guidance. But she still misses Fran. Having been so closely connected for the first thirty years of their lives, Gail is still adapting to her new status.

I never in a million katrillion years thought that she would be living in a completely different city. Our whole life I just thought we'd be up the street from each other and that our kids would be best friends. But they are. We've been very good at making sure our kids are close and that we still are close, and we see each other as much as we can. But even after all this time, I still get upset when I think, "Why did she have to go? Why?" But on the other hand, I like our situation. And I love the fact that she's only a six-hour drive away and I can go see her whenever I want.

"I Would Achieve More without Him, But I Love Him So Much"—Victor's Story

Victor and his twin brother, Howard, are in their midthirties. They are both single, live in adjoining houses, and are extremely close. A few years ago, Howard had to leave town on business for about three months. Victor felt terribly lost without his brother but also realized something about being separated from Howard: he made a lot more progress on the various projects he was pursuing. Victor freelances in a creative field, and his productivity depends on self-discipline. When Howard was out of town, Victor became much more energized and focused. This was how he explained the effect Howard's absence had on his work:

> I was lost and lonely when Howie left. But when I got used to it I became very productive because I am lazy when he is around. As soon as he got back, it was over—I stopped putting all that time and energy into my work. Without my brother I know I would be more focused on what I want to do, so he is a setback in that way. If I am home and working, and he calls, I will stop and go do something with him like go surfing, or play video games. I guess it boils down to—I would rather play with Howard than work.

The brothers have been having fun together all their lives, so it is understandable that Victor would not want to give that up, even as a mature man in his thirties. He told me that when they were kids and one of them got into trouble, their mom would have to punish both of them because they were always in collusion. The boys also spoke their own secret language when they were young, not unusual for twins. As adults they still communicate through a kind of shortcut language of their own, which Victor claims is an amazing benefit when the two are working on a project together:

> Howie knows my ideas almost without my having to speak. I'll say two words and he'll understand exactly what I wanted. He can read my mind and knows what I'm aiming for—gets it right away. No one else would get what I mean in two words. I feel weaker when he is not around.

Being on the same wavelength with his brother can be advantageous when the two are working on a project together. The downside is that Victor seems unwilling to give anyone else except his brother the opportunity to partner with him because he knows the communication won't go as smoothly. And then there is the fact that Howard's presence interrupts Victor's creative flow as often as it enhances it. Victor recognizes that his twin's interference in his workday is often a handicap, a "setback" as he put it; however, he also enjoys the fun they have together—and is unable to postpone it even when he knows he should. Perhaps Victor's continued reticence about separating his life from Howard's even minimally is rooted not only in the brothers' closeness growing up but in a particular incident that took place when they were eleven. Victor explained:

> On our eleventh birthday, Howard was in the hospital for a blood infection, and I was not allowed in his room because they were afraid I could get infected too. I forced my mom to buy a small car to give to him, and I remember standing outside his room watching him play with the car. There was a glass between us and we looked at each other and it was the saddest day of my life not being able to be with him. I have not spent any birthday or Christmas apart since then. I know we are two separate beings and should want that separation, but I don't know if I want that because we are so close. He is my best friend and my everything.

Howard is not only Victor's best friend; he is basically his only friend—and it has been that way since they were children. "I feel like a weird person," he said, "because of the way we relate and don't have other friends. We never needed anyone else. We couldn't wait for our friends to leave us alone; they were interfering with us."

The brothers have remained virtually inseparable, and Victor continues to overlook, even deny, the burden that this overly close relationship places on him. He told me that if Howard comes over while he's working, he often has to find something to occupy his brother so that he can get some work done. I asked Victor to consider how he would feel if he could devote more time to his creative work without having to worry about Howard. If he didn't have to sacrifice his goals because he feels bad about abandoning Howard, would he feel relieved or liberated? Victor responded that he doesn't consider the time he spends with his brother a sacrifice.

The intense pull Victor feels toward Howard might be odd to a nontwin, but it is not that uncommon among twins, and it is very real for Victor. At one point, he described his need to be with Howard as an "addiction":

> I would rather feel guilty about not working than give up time with him. I feel like a void if he's not home, like there's something missing. It's like an addiction. The real thing is that I am happy to give up working to spend time with him. That pleases me more. It is not a sacrifice.

Victor told me about a recurring dream he has had in which he is engaged in some activity but is surprised that Howard is not there. For example, he said, "I dream of going on a surfing trip on a tropical island and he is not there. But if I were to go for real I would not go without him because I am not able to enjoy anything if he is not there." Perhaps in his dream Victor is testing how it might feel to take part in something he enjoys without Howard's presence. Of course it would be different or surprising to be enjoying himself as an individual. But maybe on some level he is ready to do just that.

Victor said he wants to get married and have a family but is worried about how this would affect his relationship with Howard. So far the brothers have not allowed relationships with women to interfere with their twinship, but Victor admits that Howard has accused him of being jealous of Howard's current girlfriend. In fact, Victor wonders whether he will be able to "let go" of Howard once his brother becomes more serious with a woman. And he wonders, too, about his own future. Will he be able to devote himself to a wife and family if that means diminishing his relationship with Howard? Victor expressed his concerns about all of these issues:

> I don't see myself trying to hold my brother back from the person that he loves—and I realize that the greatest love is being able to let him go. That shows more love than keeping him close. Will I be able to do that?

I never give priority to my girlfriends—never. And even though I can't wait to have a wife and kids and become a dad, I want my brother to be there when I do. I would still want him as a very close part of my life. Will I ever be able to love a wife more than my brother? That's a big conflict. I know it's a different kind of love, but if I had to ask "Who would you rather throw down a cliff?" it would not be my brother. It is too big a question to grasp.

Victor seems to want such big questions to resolve themselves without his having to make any big changes. Unable to determine how he and his brother can become less dependent on each other yet still remain close, he described his current mental state—and that of his brother—as "in limbo." He wants the chance to "try life without having him around" yet he cannot seem to make the first move. He described his current challenge in the following way:

If something is meant to be to make us go apart, that's one thing. But from our side, it will never happen because we would not let it happen. We are in limbo. Our lives depend upon each other so much that we don't want to be without each other, even if we could. Will I feel weird if I'm still unmarried at fifty-five? Yes. And I would regret not having a wife or a child. But sometimes I think I will never get married. I would have to be dedicated to her and have space from my brother, and I cannot really imagine it even though I really want it. If Howie were to marry, I would feel a void.

Sometimes I wish he were not there so I could be on my own. I'm tempted to try life without having him around and I fantasize about taking the risk to be without him, but that's not likely to happen. Although I wish it would so I could see what it might be like.

Victor's ambivalence is apparent. He fantasizes about becoming independent from Howard yet cannot imagine having "space from my brother." How might Victor take the first step toward creating that space? He could begin by setting boundaries with Howard. He could let his brother know that his work is important to him, that he needs to focus on it during certain periods, and that it would be best if Howard didn't come over at those times. By carving out a block of time that is completely his own, Victor can become accustomed to working without interruptions from his brother. Regardless of the fact that he enjoys those interruptions and the fun he has with his brother, Victor may begin to develop a better relationship with himself once he has time to focus on his own needs and pursuits.

"I Would Have Loved to Have Had a Road Map for How to Create Your Own Identity"—Nancy's Story

Nancy was nearly thirty years old before deciding to live separately from her twin sister, Tamara. The two had attended the same college, where they lived together until they graduated. They spent about a year apart but then attended graduate schools in the same city, again sharing an apartment. In her midtwenties, Nancy started to see a therapist for what she thought were relationship issues with her boyfriend. During therapy, she uncovered the fact that her conflict stemmed in part from her overly close relationship to her twin. Nancy explained:

> I realized that it was just the whole breaking away from my twin relationship that had to be dealt with. And I'll never forget, in the middle of ranting at Tamara about our clashing living habits—because she had piles of junk everywhere and it would drive me crazy—I said, "I think I need to move out. I think we need to get our own space." And she agreed with that.

In addition to the "piles of junk" argument, there was an even more influential event that motivated Nancy to finally decide to get her own place. She and Tamara attended an annual twins festival. Witnessing hundreds of pairs of adult twins dressed exactly alike and extolling the virtues of twindom touched a nerve with Nancy:

> We were in our late twenties at the time, and one evening they had a kickoff party before the festival began, and we had the chance to meet a bunch of twins that were around our age or older. And I think it

was an epiphany for the two of us that there were twins who were in their fifties, sixties, seventies—and their only relationship was with each other. And I was like, "That's not healthy!" I said to my sister, "We have to work on this!" We had actually looked at a couple of books and articles on individuating, and I really worked hard with my therapist at the time, and my sister had as well. We really believed that in order for us to have more successful relationships outside of our twinship, we had to get it together and live more separate lives.

As a result the sisters decided to break the news to their parents. While it would seem like a perfectly natural decision for two young professional women to live apart, in the eyes of Nancy and Tamara's parents, it was a terrible plan. Nancy explained:

> So we went to dinner with my parents, and I'll never forget telling them, "Listen, I'm going to move to the Westside," which is like fifteen minutes away from Tamara, and you would have thought I'd said, "I'm going to shoot my sister." I mean, it was so funny. They said, "Oh my, God, that's fiscally irresponsible. You're supposed to stay together and take care of each other!" I remember saying to my parents, "No. I'm twenty-eight! I don't want my twin sister to be my only close relation-ship!" Within a month, I moved out, moved into my own apartment and Tamara stayed in the other apartment. And I'm telling you, the first week we were like, "Hey, this is the best thing for us!"

But moving out wasn't the only challenge Nancy had to face in her quest to lead a more independent life. In their midthirties, Tamara got married and had two children. Nancy was still single. Tamara assumed that Nancy would take on the role of substitute parent—or at least weekend baby-sitter. Nancy had other ideas.

> Tamara's expectation was that after her and her husband, I would be second in line—because we look alike, we talk alike, we probably would raise children similarly. And I was very close with her kids and very willing to give my time to baby-sit or to help her out in a

moment's notice. Until it started to get frustrating. Because I was like, "I'm not baby-sitting for you on a Friday night. I have a social life!"

And then when I planned to move to a new neighborhood, she didn't want me to move. And I told her, "I want to live where all my friends are, and where my life is, and so I'm not living closer to you just to be your caretaker." And she really was very, very upset. She told me, "You moved so far away!" But I made it crystal-clear that Auntie Nancy is not the only baby-sitter. I mean, I love those kids, and I will help them out as much as I can, but I am not there to be the third in command.

Tamara was openly frustrated with Nancy at first, and the two had many arguments over Nancy's move and her unwillingness to become the on-call baby-sitter. Tamara thought Nancy was being selfish; Nancy thought Tamara was being inconsiderate. And for weeks the two found it hard to relate to each other. But throughout her years of transition from Tamara's live-in roommate and companion to her independent life as a single, professional woman, Nancy had honestly and forcefully stated her position: she wanted to have her own apartment, she wanted to live in a neighborhood that fit her single lifestyle, and she did not want to become her sister's weekend child-care provider. I told Nancy she should feel proud for setting the boundaries with Tamara, that she had honestly expressed her feelings and set the limits of their relationship. It takes courage to separate your life from your twin's after so many years of living as a quasi couple. When I asked Nancy how she had managed to pull it off, she responded:

> It took me a while to come into my own. I was not the most secure person. It wasn't until after I went through graduate school, where I did really well, and then started to build my career and meet some like-minded friends, and did a very rigorous spiritual journey at that time as well, that I gained more confidence. And then in my late twenties I finally got it, and it was like, "Wait a minute, this is not right. This is not working for us. We need to have our own lives."
>
> I always fell into the same pattern of being the cared-for one, my sister being bossy. So it wasn't until I had those tools that I had the

confidence to say, "This is the path that I'm taking." Whether my sister had always assumed she had that role of decision maker, or I allowed that to happen, she was definitely the stronger personality. And now I think we're on equal ground.

Nancy was happy to offer her story knowing that other adult twins might benefit from her experiences. She told me that she wished she had been able to read something when she was younger that would have provided guidance about how to separate from your twin while preserving a healthy, loving relationship. She put it this way:

> Even though we're both fairly independent now and very successful and what have you, I would have loved to have had a little bit of a road map of how to not damage your relationship as a twin, but how to create your own identity at a younger age. Because I think that would have helped both of us.

Signs That You May Need More Separation from Your Twin

In interviewing adult twins for this book, people often said they were having certain problems in their twinship—or in their life in general—that they didn't fully understand. A young woman wondered why she became increasingly irritated with her twin over seemingly trivial issues. A man in his thirties couldn't see the connection between his panic attacks and his twin brother's impending marriage. What I explored with these individuals, and many others, was how a lack of separateness from your twin can have consequences ranging from irritability and anger to depression and, in the case of one interviewee, attempted suicide.

When you haven't had the opportunity to experience life as an individual, you don't have the chance to form a secure sense of who you truly are. The constant presence of your twin can be both an irritant and a security blanket. On some level you may sense the need to separate, but rather than make that happen, you may find yourself getting upset with him or her for almost no reason. Or, you may be aware of the fact that your lives are overly connected, but when your twin takes steps to separate you may develop panic attacks.

The following comments from various interviewees indicate the need to create more space between oneself and one's twin. Perhaps you will find that some of these experiences and feelings mirror your own.

- "All our fights are really about nothing, but we know how to get to each other where it hurts the most."

- "I want to tell her to go find her own friends and stop homing in on mine!"

- "When he got engaged, I joked around saying he had somebody and I didn't. But then I got pretty mad and started lashing out in anger."

- "We brought out the worst in each other."

- "I feel mean because my twin is too clingy and wants to hug all the time and I told her I don't want to."

- "You can love your twin as much as you can hate him."

- "I'm tired of this relationship . . . we are too true to each other."

Feeling that you bring out the worst in each other or that you hate your twin as often as you love him or her are not signs of a healthy relationship. Fighting with your same-age sibling occasionally is normal, but lashing out in anger upon hearing that your twin is engaged, or arguing constantly for no good reason may signal a need to create more space between the two of you. It is important to recognize that fighting with your twin may be a way to get distance from each other, a way to separate from each other by expressing—albeit in an angry way—that you feel very differently from him or her and that you are your own person.

Every person wants to experience his or her individuality. As twins, you may love each other and feel extremely connected to one another, but if you haven't had the opportunities for separateness you won't be able to feel comfortable within yourself as a unique person. So I encourage you to create those opportunities. For example, make social plans that do not include your twin, attend an event or class by yourself, or introduce yourself to new acquaintances without mentioning that you have a twin. These new experiences will help you discover who you are apart from your sibling.

Guidelines for Dealing with Separation Blues

Separating and individuating from your twin is a slow and gradual process. It requires patience, understanding, and empathy. Be kind to yourself as you acknowledge your own needs and attempt to deflect or dismiss your twin's disapproval or hostility.

- Acknowledge that creating a more independent life may not be easy at first, but it will be tremendously liberating and lead to personal growth.

- Expect your twin to feel rejected, hurt, or angry at the beginning of this journey.

- Learn to set limits and create boundaries with your twin by gently and clearly articulating why you need time apart.

- If you cannot manage to separate from your twin or are having difficulty in the process, consider seeking help from a therapist who is trained to understand twinship issues.

5

Comparing the Pair of You

She always seemed to do everything before me. I watched her and performed the same thing after her. This pattern has continued throughout my life so far. My twin would always accomplish things before I would; she would always be one step ahead of me in everything.
—Olivia, 22

When my twin brother came out, I felt like I was alone for the first time in my life. I was disturbed and depressed for almost a month. I had anxiety and upsetting dreams and I was grossed out listening to him flirt with guys on the phone. I also felt that he had one-upped me because he had finally struck out on his own and identified himself as different from me.
—Max, 35

It is not unusual for adult siblings to compare themselves to one another, to measure their strengths and weaknesses and successes and failures against those of their sister or brother. After all, they come from the same immediate family so, all things being equal, their lives should be pretty much on a par. Of course, their paths are rarely if ever equal—even when siblings are twins. But with twins there is the added assumption that one twin's life path will never diverge very far from the other's, and that any twists and turns along the way will be slight. This unrealistic expectation can result in endless comparisons: from whose job is more prestigious or lucrative to whose children are more over- or underweight.

In this chapter, we'll explore why adult twins continue to struggle with the issue of comparisons and differences. While it may seem obvious that at any given stage in life, one or the other twin will be happier, luckier, or healthier than the other, learning to accept that such differences are normal is not always easy for same-age siblings. Just as Max found it difficult to accept his twin brother's sexual orientation, other adult twins highlighted in this chapter struggled with comparison-related issues, including the following:

- Feeling alienated from your twin because his/her life is now so different from yours

- Feeling guilty when your accomplishments outshine those of your twin

- Feeling as if you are constantly in your twin's shadow

- Feeling resentful because your twin hasn't had to confront the hardships you've endured

- Feeling annoyed with parents, relatives, and friends who continue to compare you and your twin

The key to tolerating differences between you and your twin is developing a stronger sense of self. When your identity is based on who you know yourself to be, apart from your twin, you won't be offended by comparisons, nor will you look to your twin for an accurate measure of your worth or well-being. As you read about other adult twins who have confronted the issues of comparison and differences, you may recognize how you have been similarly affected by your twinship. Throughout this chapter we will explore how you can deal with these issues by learning more about yourself and becoming your own person.

"She Was Always One Step Ahead of Me"—Olivia's Story

Twenty-two-year-old Olivia told me that she and her "older" identical twin sister, Kendra, used to be very close. Growing up, they were "best friends and worst enemies—and always competitive." But from what Olivia described, the competition was essentially one-sided as Kendra "always won, because she always had better grades than me, she looked prettier, and had more friends." Olivia feels she has been engaged in an endless—and hopeless—pursuit of Kendra's higher academic and social standing. She characterized their twinship hierarchy in simple, yet self-deprecating terms:

> When we were kids, she was baby A, I was baby B. She was the angel, I was bozo. She always seemed to do everything before me, and I watched her and performed the same thing after her. This pattern has continued throughout my life so far. She would always accomplish things before I would, she would always be one step ahead of me in everything.

Olivia then elaborated:

> I was the younger twin. I was the shorter twin, and for some reason I was the more competitive one. She naturally would do a lot better than me in athletics and different clubs we were in, so I always felt like it was a competition, with me trying to do as well as Kendra. Academic-wise, she had straight As, except for senior year when she got one B. I was always struggling to get As and Bs. I only got one C in high school, but for me it was always frustrating that I could never quite reach what she did.

At this point in our interview, Olivia started to cry. Her sense of defeat and hopelessness was apparent as she continued, telling me how the sisters' college application process became yet another contest. And again, Kendra was the winner.

> We applied to the same five colleges. My sister had the better grades and better SAT score, so she got into all five. I only got into three. Unfortunately, the two colleges that I didn't get into were my top

choices. Kendra not only made it into a better school, but of course she made it into the college I wanted to go to, so yet again she "won" in my mind. She was better than me in everything.

When she got to college, Olivia started seeing a counselor for her depression. Olivia learned what is now obvious to her: that a lot of her low self-esteem issues stemmed from feeling inferior to her twin, whom she still refers to as "my older identical twin."

Because Olivia has always compared herself to her sister, she has never measured herself by her own standards. If she had, she would have appreciated the indisputable facts: her grades were excellent and her extracurricular life and social standing were admirable as well, given that she had been elected president of her favorite high school club. But Olivia continued to see herself in her sister's shadow and is still having a hard time stepping out of it.

Attending separate colleges offered an opportunity for Olivia to be on her own, discover her own academic interests, and make her own friends. Olivia said that it was easy to make friends during freshman year because everyone was just starting out and anxious to form new connections. But during her second year, some of the friendships started to dissipate. Meanwhile, Olivia said, Kendra was doing just fine:

> A lot of my friends from freshman year no longer liked me or just faded away, and then Kendra started making more and more friends, even though it was really difficult for her at first. So it was quite opposite, and I got jealous of her. Eventually, I didn't have any friends and she started gaining a lot of friends. So we were different.

The fact that she is "opposite" and different from her sister has always contributed to Olivia's negative self-image. There is the sense that because she doesn't measure up to her sister in countless ways, she is less than Kendra, even the mirror opposite. She sees herself as the "B" to Kendra's "A." But what if she could view herself as a stand-alone individual? Might Olivia come to appreciate all the positive qualities she possesses, all the effort she has put into her studies, and the determination she now exemplifies as she pursues the career she envisions for herself? Unfortunately, like many twins Olivia can't give up the twin comparison game because it is played not just by her parents and friends but by our culture. Nearly every twin I speak with tells me how tired he is of being referred to as "the creative one" or "the studious one," "the outgoing one" or "the shy one." Constantly being labeled, typecast, pigeon-holed, and judged in comparison to your twin, rather than perceived as an individual like everyone else, robs you of your singular identity.

Olivia is trying to recast the vision she has of herself so that it reflects her own passions and personality and accomplishments. Spending four years at college away from Kendra made her realize she is more than just her sister's twin. Still, she admits she is "struggling with trying to find my own identity." Olivia remembers too well the discomfort she felt when people used to grill her about being a twin. At the time, she didn't have the perspective on her twinship she has now, so she couldn't articulate an appropriate response. However, she was able to explain to me what she wishes nontwins could understand:

> As a twin growing up, I always hated when people said, "Oh, what is it like being a twin? I wish I had a twin!" And we'd be like, "No, you don't wish you had a twin. Don't say that!" In a way it was a positive thing, but it is much tougher being a twin than a lot of people think. It is hard being a twin because we were constantly being compared to each other by others. It's like people sometimes don't realize we actually both have our own feelings and personalities; we're not just one collective. We're our own selves, and I wish people would realize that.

The Myth of Mirror Opposites

Authentic differences between twins are a good thing, but contrived differences such as "the good one" and "the bad one" (or the "angel" and the "bozo," as Olivia put it) signify that each twin is being defined in relationship to the other—rather than being considered on his or her own terms. And such designations are often far from accurate. For example, Twin A might be sociable in most circumstances but because Twin B is more gregarious, Twin A gets stuck with "the shy one" label. If Twin A has a good singing voice as a child, she may be referred to as "our musical twin" while Twin B gets called "our athlete"—even though Twin B may have stronger capabilities as a future musician.

Obviously, it can be detrimental for parents of twins to label their twins in this way. Not only might they be confining their children to roles that can easily change as each twin develops, but they are teaching their twins that each of them will always be measured against the other.

Sometimes the "mirror opposite phenomenon" is instigated by one or both twins. In fact, it is not uncommon for twins who have been enmeshed or overly close to go to exaggerated lengths to attempt to differentiate themselves. This often happens during adolescence. For example, one twin will deliberately hang out with the bad crowd or engage in self-destructive, risky behavior simply to be distinguished from his or her same-age sibling. Or one twin will avoid an activity she enjoys because the other twin is involved in it, and instead choose something that is unattractive to the other twin. This urgent need to develop a division between the two is often the result of twins not having had the opportunity to become individuated as children.

As an adult, it can be very limiting to think of yourself as your twin's mirror opposite. When you define yourself in terms of what your same-age sibling is *not*, you are hanging on to outdated childhood labels, which may have been inaccurate to begin with. Don't you both deserve to be acknowledged for the complex, nuanced individuals you have become—without any reference to your shared birthday? Mirror opposite characters work well in myths, fairy tales, and good guy–bad guy movies, but they don't reflect the real lives of same-age siblings.

"I Feel Guilty When I Do Well and He Struggles"—Peter's Story

A common theme among adult twins is that comparisons between the two can leave one twin feeling guilty. Since twins often grow up believing they are essentially equal, they expect that their adult lives will be fairly equal as well. But when one twin does better financially, has a happier marriage, or has fewer life challenges, he may not feel entitled to fully enjoy such benefits because his twin doesn't enjoy them as well. On the one hand, a twin's guilt can be seen as compassionate since it embodies a sensitive, caring approach toward one's same-age sibling. But is it realistic to expect that one twin's life will be parallel to the other's? The fact is that even though twins are born on the same day to the same parents, each of their lives will deviate from the other's in myriad ways; this is as it should be. Sometimes, however, that reality can be difficult to accept, as Peter's story attests.

Peter told me that "overall, being a twin is the greatest thing that's ever happened to me." Now thirty-two, he and his brother, Richard, attended the same college but have been living in separate cities for the last six years. Peter said that living apart was a way for each of them to "have our own lives." The two have a good relationship and talk on the phone almost every day. The brothers have always known they had very different personalities and inclinations. Still, Peter can't help but be sensitive about their differences. When he explained how they differed in high school, Peter was careful not to imply that Richard's social standing was any less than his, even though he mentioned that Richard may have been "living in my shadow sometimes":

> In high school, Richard and I had somewhat different friends. He was
> a little bit more of a wise guy and kind of made a name for himself
> as the wise-ass twin. I think over time he maybe thought that he was
> kind of the less-liked twin. Not in an overwhelmingly bad way. He
> was fine; he wasn't like an unhappy kid in high school or anything like

that, but I just feel like he was kind of living in my shadow sometimes, even though he really had no reason to feel that way.

Almost apologetically, Peter said that after high school and throughout their twenties he became increasingly more successful than Richard. In the last several years, as Peter's career took off, Richard's began to decline. Richard lost his job due to the poor economy and according to Peter has been struggling to "catch back up to where he was." Peter felt bad about the economic discrepancy between him and his brother and was unsure how to be supportive of Richard without appearing to be superior or preachy. Peter was also concerned that being "ahead of" his twin meant he was negating the expectation that the brothers should be identical. Peter explained:

> I did become successful, ahead of him in a sense. I was definitely working hard for it, but I do feel that in a way he's looked at my life and thought, "Okay, my twin brother is kind of ahead of me." So that's one of the more difficult aspects about being a twin. And if I try and give him advice, I can't help but feel that guilt that I'm lecturing to him or something. And I kind of get the sense that he feels that way because why would he want to hear life advice from someone who's supposed to be identical to him? He would automatically get put off by it.

Peter's sensitivity toward his brother's situation leaves him not only feeling guilty about his own success but also worried about how to communicate with Richard. He is afraid of offending his brother or coming across as bossy, yet he wants to be helpful. As with many twins, Peter has the ability to read Richard's emotions; he is aware of how Richard is feeling without Richard expressing his feelings in words. When I asked him if he and Richard had ever directly addressed the subject of their career differences, Peter said:

> I might be telling him something positive about my job and I'll sense something in his voice when he says, "Oh man, you just got another good job . . ." and I'll say, "Well, why do you sound upset about that?

You should be happy," and he'll say, "No, no, I am, but I wish I could find a job like that," or something like that. So we have had those conversations, and at the end of it he knows he just needs to get something done for himself. He deals with that little bit of jealousy as it happens, but it hasn't been overwhelmingly negative for him. So, we've addressed it but it is not something that we talk about all the time.

Peter told me he wants to be able to talk to his brother "so that he doesn't feel threatened and I won't feel guilty for having success before him." He puts himself in Richard's shoes by adding that their situation may be reversed at some point. "If my twin was having certain successes and I wasn't," he said, "I know I'd feel more upset about it than if it was just a friend. But I would want to know that it is okay for one of us to be doing better than the other."

Many twins grapple with the inequality issue, even as they acknowledge that they are individuals leading their own lives. Like Peter, they struggle to believe it's okay for one to be doing better than the other or for one to experience something before the other twin has. As much as Peter would like for his brother to be doing better at the moment, he knows that it doesn't make sense for the two of them to have equal experiences in life. Life doesn't work that way, even for twins. But as sensitive and smart as Peter is, he still has to convince himself that the inequality between twins is inevitable. Here is his comment on the subject:

> That's the only thing that's kind of touchy regarding my twin and I: how to deal with one twin either doing worse or better—and how to deal with one twin experiencing things in life before the other twin. I mean, someone's going to have kids first and someone's going to get married first, and someone's going to become financially stable first or buy a house first.

I told Peter that instead of feeling guilty about his achievements, he should feel proud of them and proud of the fact he has been a good role model for his brother. While Peter's accomplishments have sometimes discouraged Richard, they have also inspired him. Peter told me that "it does suck for Richard sometimes to hear that I'm doing well, but at other times it kind of keeps him going because he realizes that 'If my brother is successful, then I could be successful.'"

Peter cannot change Richard's circumstances. Richard must do that himself. Fortunately, Peter is not the kind of sibling who makes his brother feel bad for not matching up to his own success. Nor does Peter convey that he is in any way disappointed in Richard. To the contrary, Peter strives to consistently validate and encourage his brother. And it is obvious that he loves him very much. When I commented that Richard is lucky to have a caring brother like Peter, Peter responded: "I'm lucky to have him, too. He helps me out in plenty of ways, too."

The Fear of Twin Differences

Although inequities between siblings exist in every family, with twins those differences can strike at the heart of the twinship, causing some adult twins to worry that their relationship will be in danger if one person's life becomes starkly dissimilar from the other's. The following comments from survey respondents reveal this concern:

- "If I have more children, it will lead her to resent me more."—29-year-old female

- "I used to feel my twin had to do as well as me, and that held me back."—33-year-old male

- "My twin and I are obese. I would like to lose the weight but I don't want us to look unidentical."—26-year-old female

- "I don't want to have a serious relationship with a woman because my brother doesn't have anyone."—30-year-old male

- "We have to agree on things, not little things but big issues. I think it's because we don't want to be different."—24-year-old female

It is an incredible burden to have to lead your life according to how your actions will affect your sibling. Yet twins such as those quoted above willingly take on that responsibility because they fear the consequences of being too different from their same-age sibling. Among the feared outcomes are these: the closeness to your twin will be shattered, your twin will be emotionally damaged, and you will be unable to enjoy your success because your twin will not be sharing in it. Holding oneself back from succeeding in a career, losing weight, finding a mate, or having children—because you don't want to jeopardize your sibling relationship—would seem bizarre to nontwins. But maintaining twin equality is a kind of unwritten promise between many same-age siblings. Is this a promise you intend to keep throughout your life, regardless of how it interferes with what you want to accomplish or enjoy?

The key to overcoming a fear of twin differences is to acknowledge your right to own your life and to make choices based on your own goals and desires. If you have never had the opportunity to discover who you are apart from your twin, this process can be challenging. But once you feel entitled to be your own person, you'll be able to make those individual choices. And in doing so, you'll be able to live without the guilt and without second-guessing how your twin will react to your decisions.

Those life decisions are yours to make, and you deserve to make them on your own.

"I Was Deteriorating While Yasmine Was Becoming More and More Beautiful"—Sophie and Yasmine's Story

It is one thing to feel guilty because you're enjoying a successful career while your twin is struggling, but what if your twin has a life-threatening disease and you are perfectly healthy? When one twin has a serious medical problem, the twinship may be affected in a variety of ways. The healthy twin may feel guilty that she is the one who was spared. She may take on a caretaker role or intensify that role if she already held it. She may fear she will inherit the affliction. Or she may distance herself from her twin to avoid the inherent pain and distress. As for the ill twin, she may feel resentful for having been singled out as the one to suffer. She may expect her twin to assume more of a caretaking role. Or she may feel more distant from her twin because the two have become dissimilar in such a fundamental way.

When Sophie was diagnosed with cancer at the age of thirteen, she and her twin sister, Yasmine, experienced several of these emotional consequences. Now eighteen years old, the two are beginning to understand the changes forced upon their twinship during Sophie's illness.

From early on, Sophie and Yasmine had very distinct personalities but were always close. Yasmine described Sophie as gutsy, brave, and protective:

> When we were younger, Sophie was the one who got her shot at the doctor first, and later on, she got her ears pierced before me. She was so rebellious. She started wearing makeup in the seventh grade, even when our mom told her not to, and I'd be thinking, "Oh, am I supposed to wear makeup, too?" But she's always stood up for me. She would put herself in danger before she would let something happen to me.

Sophie tended to take the lead socially, making friends who would then become friends of both sisters. Yasmine depended on Sophie to be the leader—the strong, confident sister. And then one day, in the course of their yearly check-up, the doctor discovered a lump in Sophie's abdomen, which turned out to be a tumor. Yasmine recalled the series of events that followed:

> We were freaking out, and Sophie ended up not going to camp that summer. She had surgery while I was at camp. Then it was fine, but she kept worrying that the cancer was going to come back. One day we were out shopping, and she had to sit down all the time because she was so tired. None of us wanted to believe that anything was wrong and that she would be fine. But she wasn't. She needed chemotherapy for six months and countless surgeries.

As for Sophie, the shock of having cancer at such a young age, along with the fear of what lay ahead and the ordeal of her treatments, were only part of her experience. She was also harboring some distressing feelings about her relationship with Yasmine, which she described in the following way:

> Being a twin made that experience unusual for me. I found myself becoming frustrated that I was deteriorating while Yasmine was becoming more and more beautiful. We were always supposed to be the same, progressing at the same speed, but she hit puberty and blossomed and I turned into a little kid again. Every day I compared myself to her. It wasn't just that I was missing out on being a teenager. I felt that I was far behind her and she kept going and going.

Sadly, Sophie's suffering was compounded when she compared herself to Yasmine. It should have been a time when *both* girls began to blossom, but instead, Sophie felt she was being left "far behind." As with others profiled in this chapter, Sophie expected that her experiences would be very similar to her same-age sibling's. But having those expectations so harshly denied created the sense that life was not unfolding as it should. To complicate matters further, Yasmine turned to Sophie's ex-boyfriend for solace, leaving Sophie feeling isolated and betrayed. Sophie explained:

> I had a boyfriend for a couple of weeks before my first seizure. It wasn't anything serious—more like a teenage crush. We broke up and Yasmine went to him for comfort during my treatment. He ended up being her source of support, and she distanced herself from me, falling into his arms instead of mine. I became furious that during my time of deepest need, she was with my ex-boyfriend, whom she ended up dating for three years. It's not that I was mad she ended up dating him. It's that I felt betrayed at a time when I needed her to be loyal. I didn't really understand what she was going through. I just knew I was hurt by the person I cared about the most.

Five years later, Yasmine now admits she probably distanced herself from Sophie because she was scared. She realizes her thinking was irrational, but she was scared she was going to get sick, too. At thirteen, she reasoned that if one twin has cancer, the other has a good chance of getting it as well. When they spoke about it recently, Yasmine told Sophie what she had been feeling at the time. This is how she described their conversation:

> I told Sophie that I had been scared I was going to have cancer, too. She said that at the time, she really didn't understand why I had pulled away from her, but she was mad—she felt I kind of checked out. And I said, "No! It is because I was so scared I was gonna get sick."

Of course, Yasmine was scared for herself, but she was scared for Sophie, too. Watching your sister suffer through a serious illness would be devastating for anyone, especially for such a young person. As for Sophie's ex-boyfriend, Yasmine had this to say:

> He was her boyfriend for a week, like the first week of school. But six months later, he and I ended up going out for a really long time. And Sophie was fine with that. I think I trusted him because she did. I know that's kind of messed up.

It makes sense that Yasmine trusted the boyfriend because Sophie had; it was another instance of her following Sophie's lead. But an interesting change took place for Yasmine during the period when Sophie was so sick: she came out of her shell. For the first time in her life, Yasmine was on her own, without her more-confident sister leading the way. She hung out with her friends as an individual and held her own socially. Granted, these were friendships Sophie had initiated, but without Sophie, Yasmine felt more independent. When she admitted this to me, she said she felt somewhat guilty about it:

> I think when I was little, I felt a little bit in her shadow. So when she was sick, it was the one time I wasn't really in her shadow in school. And it's so weird to say that because it shouldn't be a good thing.

I explained to Yasmine that during the difficult period of her sister's illness, she had thrived in a way she could not have done before. And it was okay for her to acknowledge that. Of course, Yasmine never would have wished for Sophie to get sick, nor did she think it was "a good thing," but it was good that Yasmine could look back on her experience of being more independent and know it was a healthy change for her. Her separation from Sophie gave her the space to be herself.

While Yasmine was discovering her individuality, Sophie was experiencing the most difficult years of her young life. How did the sisters' extremely different experiences affect Sophie? Sophie said she was hurt and resentful that Yasmine had pulled away from her during her illness. She held on to that resentment for several years until she came to a profound realization while volunteering at a summer camp for children suffering with cancer:

> I was a counselor for kids whose siblings have cancer. I remember thinking, "These aren't the kids I came to help. I came for the patients afflicted with problems—they're the ones who really need me!" But being with the siblings, it hit me like a train how much they were affected by watching their siblings go through something terrifying. I had a conversation with a little girl whose brother was going through chemotherapy, and she explained to me how her life and her family's completely revolve around him—and how it made her feel to watch her brother become weaker and weaker. My campers were constantly worried about their siblings and developed a sort of parent-type relationship. This reminded me of Yasmine so much because she's always worried about me now.

Sophie's experience of being with these children was so intense that she became emotionally overwhelmed and had to leave the camp sooner than planned. She then began to rethink how it must have been for Yasmine during the initial years of Sophie's illness.

> I cried for hours every day because for the first time I realized how it must have been for my sister to watch me dying—thinking that if she came near me or shared my clothes she would get cancer too, because why wouldn't she? Her thinking was that we share our genes,

we shared a womb, we shared the exact same life—so why was I the one that got sick? She didn't understand why she was healthy and I wasn't. I had thought that I was the one going downhill while she was rising up, but talking to my campers I realized that being the sibling is much worse, much more scarring. For a twin, watching someone who is supposed to be your other half become less and less of a person will forever haunt the person who has to watch.

Sophie is healthy now and enjoying her friends and her studies, and Yasmine is in college and still adjusting to being her own person, apart from Sophie. Yasmine worries about Sophie's health but is just as concerned about her own ongoing process of individuation. Both sisters realize that their vastly different experiences as teenagers—Sophie having cancer and Yasmine remaining healthy—led them to confront their twinship. Each has a new appreciation for what the other has been through and what each must face on her own.

"When My Brother Came Out, I Felt Like I Was Alone for the First Time in My Life"—Max's Story

Although most twins want to be perceived as distinct from the other, when one becomes significantly different it may lead the other to feel threatened, disoriented, or abandoned. The difference between the two siblings might be anything from marital or economic status to religious values or, as in Max's case, sexual orientation. Since our culture holds that being a twin is essentially about sameness, when one twin deviates substantially from the other it can seem as if the twinship is in jeopardy.

When Max's brother, Frank, told him that he was gay, Max reacted with shock, outrage, and a profound sense of betrayal that reflected his deepest feelings about being a twin:

> When he first told me, I felt as if I were on drugs. I felt betrayed and abandoned. How could this be true about someone I felt I had known so well all of my life? I was totally shocked—it had never crossed my mind. At first I just thought maybe he was doing some

experimentation while he was drinking or playing out some bisexual tendencies that all of us have. But when he said that he prefers men and that he identified with being gay, I felt like I did not know who he was, that he was a stranger, and that he had been hiding something from me. I could not imagine him with a guy and felt as if I couldn't interact with him anymore. I thought, "I'll have to say good-bye to him and never be able to talk to him again."

Max likened the trauma of finding out Frank was gay to the day his father died. In both instances, Max's sense of loss was overwhelming. What he felt he had lost with Frank was the unique closeness the two had shared throughout their lives. It wasn't that the brothers had been so alike; they weren't. Frank had always been more disciplined and got better grades. Grades weren't that important to Max because he felt he had other positive traits. He was a good athlete, fair-minded yet aggressive. And people were drawn to his sense of humor. Their parents had always acknowledged each boy's strengths and differences and supported them in their separate endeavors. But as different as the brothers were, their bond had been indestructible. So why did this particular difference threaten to sever that connection? Max tried to explain:

> I felt like I was alone for the first time in my life. I was disturbed and depressed for almost a month. I had anxiety and upsetting dreams and had a difficult time listening to him flirt with guys on the tele phone. I felt alone, betrayed, and grossed out. I also felt that Frank had one-upped me because he had finally struck out on his own and identified himself as different from me. He did what he wanted to do. It is a cool thing to be able to say, "This is who I am" and to take a risk and be deviant from the mainstream and to be able to own it and flaunt it, like wearing a Mohawk. It is the ultimate expression of being different, to say, I am gay.

Max's outrage was, in part, a kind of jealousy—over the fact that Frank had succeeded in defining himself, whereas Max had not yet done so. Max's feeling that he had been "one-upped" in the struggle to be an individual is understandable. Twins often feel they are in a competition they didn't sign up for: to be the first to do something important, ahead of their twin. In Frank's case, by coming out as gay he was the first to announce to the world, "I know who I am." And in that sense, according to Max, Frank had "won."

The other piece of the story was Max's sense of abandonment. Not only was Frank's sexual identity different from Max's and therefore a potential threat to their close connection, but Frank was now becoming intimately involved with other men. Max admitted it was difficult to convince himself that he had not been replaced:

> I do not feel replaced, but it's just a little bit hard. We used to talk every day and now it is just once a week. Frank's boyfriend is amazing, and I realize that with my ex-girlfriend I had less time for Frank. So I know what it's like.

Would Max have felt as abandoned if Frank had been spending all his time with a woman instead of a man? Perhaps. But the difference in the brothers' sexual identity definitely made Max feel that their twinship was threatened, that Frank had become a stranger in a way.

Once Max had time to adjust to his brother's revelation, he felt the two of them would be able to resume a close relationship. They now live in separate cities, but Max said the distance doesn't really separate them. "Distance has nothing to do with it," he said. "We still feel connected even though we live apart and don't talk as much as we used to. I know him so well that I don't feel separate from him."

For his part, Frank was shocked that Max was not gay. He expected that because they are twins, he and Max would have the same sexual orientation. Although the presumption that twins are fundamentally alike runs counter to reality, it does not prevent twins and nontwins alike from buying into it. Much to their surprise, however, Max and Frank have learned that they don't have to be fundamentally alike to feel deeply connected.

Comparison as Inspiration—Miranda's Story

Growing up, Miranda and her twin sister, Chloe, had a lot of the same interests, but each sister excelled in different areas. Miranda was a good athlete; Chloe was not. Both girls were good artists, but according to Miranda, Chloe was more talented. As each girl pursued her studies and extracurricular activities, a competitive spirit between the two seemed to energize them both. Although there were times when one sister came in slightly behind the other, neither has ever been discouraged by comparing herself to her twin. Miranda explained:

> We graduated number one and number two in our high school
> class. I was number one, but if she had been, I would have been fine
> with that. I probably would have been a little disappointed, but we
> had this acknowledged thing where we both knew she was a better
> test-taker, but I was a more diligent student. I cared more, but on
> standardized tests Chloe always did better—and that was okay. We
> had our things that one of us was better at, and we had things that we
> were both good at.

Now in their midforties, both sisters are artists, but their subject matter is very different as are the genres in which they specialize. They encourage and support each other and are thrilled when the other is successful with a particular project. Throughout their lives they have maintained an extremely close friendship, and both admit they would be uncomfortable living too far apart. In discussing their relationship, Miranda emphasized how she has been inspired by Chloe. She said that as a wife and mother Chloe has been a crucial role model. Miranda had been reticent about taking on those life-changing roles, due to her parents' tumultuous marriage, but witnessing Chloe in her day-to-day life made all the difference. Miranda explained:

> Our parents are wonderful parents but they're not such great married
> people. So marriage was not a very appealing concept. I had very
> conflicted feelings about getting married. It was not something that
> was ever a goal of mine. So when Chloe got married, I actually took it
> as encouraging; because if she could find someone worth marrying,

then maybe I could too. She tested the waters, and I benefited from that. I thought, "Oh wow, that can work." It took me a while longer to find someone who I trusted enough.

Then, she had kids, and I have to say I was very on the fence about that—but I made a point of picking someone who wanted to have kids. And I looked at Chloe and how she dealt with her kids, and I learned a lot. It made me a lot more comfortable taking that path.

Rather than comparing herself unfavorably to Chloe and remaining stuck, Miranda saw her sister's successful family life as an inspiration. She saw that Chloe made marriage and parenting "work" and then felt more comfortable embarking on a similar path. Miranda candidly acknowledged that Chloe tends to be the more giving twin, but she is committed to becoming just as generous. Having benefited from Chloe's kindness, Miranda wants to give back in a similar way. By constructively comparing herself to Chloe and using her as a role model, Miranda is motivated to becoming more open and giving in their twinship. This is how she described it:

Chloe is really a kinder person, but I think I do try to be someone she can turn to as well. We're always each other's best critic. If she's got something she needs me to do on one of her projects, or if she needs me to baby-sit, I will drop everything. She comes first, and she knows that. We both know that we'll do that for each other. I think Chloe is emotionally more available than I am, but I'm better than I used to be.

Stop Comparing, Start Appreciating

Instead of going through life as "the X one" or "the Y one," wouldn't it be liberating to be considered on your own terms? Once you stop comparing yourself to your twin (who may have been labeled "the artistic one" or "the brainy one" at age three), you might find you are much more creative or intellectual than you give yourself credit for. Without the burden of being compared to your twin, you might finally allow yourself to strive for your own goals and fully enjoy your accomplishments. Rather than feel guilty for outshining or outperforming your twin, you might be able to see your same-age sibling in a new light and come to appreciate his or her uniqueness.

Each of us deserves to be perceived and appreciated for who we are as distinct human beings. Abandoning the comparisons to your twin brother or sister won't sever the bond between you. It will, however, help to strengthen your individuality and sense of self.

Guidelines for Seeing Your Twin
and Yourself as Individuals

If you are to begin the process of renouncing comparisons and discovering who you are as an individual—and who your twin is as well, these are essential and crucial questions to contemplate:

- If you were to meet your twin for the first time, what sort of impression would you have?

- Would you think the two of you had a lot in common?

- Which differences might strike you as particularly distinct?

- If you could think about yourself without referencing your twin, without resorting to the obligatory twin comparison game, how might you appear to yourself?

- What personal traits might you find surprising or underappreciated?

6

Seeking a Twin-like Friend or Lover

With my sister, we knew that we were both there for each other, twenty-four seven. I would drop whatever I was doing if she needed anything. So I unconsciously expected that with friends, too. It turned out, though, that I was always the need-satisfier, but never got anything back in return. —Trish, 33

There's something comforting about having someone who's that close to you, and who you can trust that much. So, yeah, that's something I still crave. —Ray, 36

Whether they are aware of it or not, adult twins may be seeking a friend or a lover who can fill the role their twin once played, as indicated in the comments above. Trish needed someone who needed her as her twin sister once had. She became involved in a string of friendships in which she was always the giver, but her overly generous acts were never reciprocated. Ray married a twin but later divorced, only to find himself longing for the intensity of a twin-like close connection. In both cases, expectations were based on having had a twin as a primary partner.

A twin's struggles within a relationship can sometimes be traced to the unconscious need to replicate the twinship. If the dynamic between you and your twin was defined by psychological dependency and that issue is not addressed, a similar dependent situation may arise in your relationships with close friends or romantic partners. If you were a caretaker to your twin, it is possible that you will seek someone with whom you can continue to fill that role. If you enjoyed a particularly close relationship with your twin, you may expect a level of closeness with friends only to be disappointed when it isn't what you'd hoped for. Or, you might enjoy an emotionally healthy twin-like relationship with a friend, lover, or spouse—based on the closeness you once had with your same-age sibling.

In this chapter, we'll hear from twins whose friendships and love affairs reflected these and other twinship-influenced scenarios:

- Expecting a friend or partner to instantly get who you are and what you need because that's how it was in your twinship

- Avoiding conflict by adapting to a friend's or lover's needs while not getting your own needs met, which may reflect the expectation that twins should always get along

- Choosing a friend or lover who will replicate either the "needy" or the "caretaker" role once filled by your twin

- Avoiding friendships for fear they may be too intrusive because you don't want to be as needy or as needed as you were in your twinship

- Establishing a close, yet emotionally healthy, friendship or intimate relationship that resembles your twinship dynamic

As you'll learn throughout this chapter, the key to dealing with these issues is to develop a stronger sense of self so that you can enter into and enjoy friendships and romantic relationships on your own terms, free of twin-related psychological baggage.

"I Dive In and Try to Get Close to Someone Way Too Soon"—Trish's Story

Trish's twin sister, Belinda, was always the first person Trish called when she needed to talk. But recently Belinda has not been as available due to her thriving social life. This has been a difficult adjustment for Trish (now in her late twenties), who has had far fewer friendships and romantic involvements than her sister. Trish explained:

> My sister and I are really different, but that's never affected how we feel about each other. I'm so used to having a close relationship with her that I tend to dive in and get close with someone way too soon. I guess I expect that same kind of instant intimacy that I had with her, and that everybody is going to be like that. And it is never like that. I'm constantly disappointed in people and how they treat me.

One of the first disappointments for Trish came during her senior year in college. She had been involved with a young man for three or four years and had essentially been his caretaker. He had ongoing emotional problems, and Trish had always been there for him. She would stay up all night talking him through his latest anxiety attack, contact his parents to assure them he was doing okay, and accompany him to family events where she provided a buffer so that he could handle being with his relatives. But after this enormous investment of her time and emotional energy, the boyfriend turned around and said, "I don't really want this relationship anymore." Trish had seen him through his problem phase, and he no longer needed or wanted her.

The caretaking role Trish had played with her boyfriend had been a replay of the role she had taken on with her twin sister, and now that neither of them needed her any longer, Trish felt lost. So she desperately attempted to create a twin connection with casual friends and acquaintances, giving of herself far beyond what was appropriate for a new friendship, and expecting love and attention in return. Trish assumed that these friendships would resemble a twin-like relationship. Since the friendship pattern in her twinship

was "If you need me, I'm on call for you twenty-four hours a day," she unconsciously applied this mind-set to potential close friends. She explained how
she had exercised poor judgment with regard to the individuals she chose
as friends and how unrealistic her expectations had been:

> I guess I have a talent for choosing selfish people, but I didn't see that
> at first. I would meet them and it would seem that they needed me,
> so I would give and give to that person. But when I needed them,
> they weren't there for me. Like this one friend, I referred her for a job,
> which she ended up getting. She appreciated that I had helped her
> out, but when I called her because I needed someone to talk to, the
> first time she was kind of nice but the second time I called she blew
> me off. It was like she was saying, "What the hell is wrong with you?"

This type of scenario was repeated a number of times before Trish and
I discussed the role she was continuing to play—and how she needed to
let it go. Certainly she had been a giving person toward her new friends,
but once she had demonstrated her generosity and thoughtfulness, she
assumed it would be reciprocated. And when it wasn't, Trish became
desperate and needy. She would make demands of the friend, and then
become terribly hurt and frustrated when she was shunned. Shattered by
rejection, she would ask me, "Why wasn't this person being nice to me
when I had been so nice to her?"

Trish is now learning that she needs to stop and think about the individual she chooses to become involved with and how she responds to that
person. I explained to her that she can teach herself to consciously evaluate
her potential friends or boyfriends and consider what the relationship is
all about, instead of "diving in" too quickly—and then being disappointed
and angry when her unrealistic expectations are not met. Rather than
setting herself up for disappointment and turning that rejection against
herself, Trish can work on developing the ability to be more perceptive
about who she's connecting with, as well as becoming more self-reflective
regarding her own motives and responses. And she can acknowledge the

degree to which her twinship has affected her unrealistic expectations of instant, unconditional intimacy.

Like Trish, twins who once filled the caretaker role in their twinship often go on to perform that emotional function within their friendships and romantic involvements. Although it may seem paradoxical, the caretaking twin feels nurtured when she takes care of the other twin. So she learns to equate caretaking with friendship and love—and getting her own needs met. But when the twinship is no longer her primary relationship (because the other twin breaks away emotionally and becomes involved with other best friends or a romantic partner), the caretaker twin suffers from not having a defining role and a sense of identity. So she looks for someone else to take care of. Since the only way she understands intimacy is to be a caretaker, when she becomes involved with a new friend or a potential partner, she tries to figure out what that person needs and how she can accommodate those needs. That is her notion of what it means to be in a loving relationship. But caretaking is not intimacy, and attaching yourself to someone who needs you is not the basis for true friendship or love. In order to become truly intimate with someone, you must have a sense of your own singularity so that you meet as equals, each giving to the other out of choice, not need.

When you have a strong sense of self—a sense of your own inner strengths, inner capacities, and inner resiliency—you're able to get through challenges without becoming overly dependent on a friend or lover. In Trish's case, she became dependent on someone needing her, in the hopes that by being a caretaker she would be loved and cared for herself. Sadly, those hopes did not materialize.

Inseparable Friends—Dylan's Story

Leo contacted me because he was worried about his twin brother, Dylan. At thirty-six, the brothers were in very different places in their lives. Leo had a career he enjoyed and was recently married. He had struggled with certain emotional issues in his twenties and early thirties, but was satis-fied that he had worked through most of them. As for Dylan, Leo told me his brother was still unsure which direction his life should take. He had worked at various jobs but had never found his calling. And he had never had a serious romantic relationship.

The brothers had been close as children, but Leo had been living in a different city for the past decade. He had kept close tabs on his brother over the years, encouraging him when he became depressed about his work and giving him pep talks over the phone to keep up his spirits. When Dylan met Dana, a woman who worked in Dylan's office, Leo was extremely relieved. At last Dylan had someone he connected with and who might become a significant other. But the relationship never went in that direction; rather, it seemed to Leo to resemble a twin-like friendship. Dana then became the encouraging partner and cheerleader for Dylan. Leo was now concerned because Dylan was about to lose Dana—his best friend with whom he had had an ongoing, intense, yet platonic relationship for the past two years. Leo worried how this loss would affect his brother:

> My brother has never had a serious sexual relationship and never
> reached his potential as far as a career goes. Our mother was kind of
> an enabler—always counseling Dylan on what he should do with his
> life. But I think that sort of backfired. Now he seems to be seriously
> stuck and feels like he's getting nowhere. At least before, he had his
> best friend to hang out with and relate to. Now she's moving away,
> and I'm really worried about him.

Leo told me he and Dylan had lived together before Leo moved away ten years ago. And he said he had essentially "spent a lifetime trying to help Dylan." Without Leo, Dylan had nearly retreated into his shell. He had never been very sociable and found it hard to meet people without Leo leading the way. But then he met Dana at work. She seemed to fill the gap created by Dylan's absence. According to Leo, Dylan and Dana became inseparable. Leo told me about a recent visit Dylan had made to Leo's home:

> The whole time he was here he was texting Dana. Dylan told me that not only did they work together, but they made their lunches together, they played volleyball together on the weekends, they did everything together. But they were sort of playing out this game and didn't want anybody at work to know that they were best friends. The thing is, there was never anything sexual about their relationship, and I think Dana finally realized after two years that it wasn't going anywhere—so she left.

As long as his brother had a partner—albeit a platonic one—Leo had been able to breathe easier. He no longer had to worry about his brother or feel bad that he didn't have "a life." But after a two-year respite from worry, Leo was now back to square one—saddled with the emotional responsibility of caretaking his twin brother. At this point, he was not only worried about Dylan, he was angry about the years he had spent agonizing over his brother's well-being. He didn't want that role anymore, which is why he turned to me for advice.

I told Leo that it seemed his brother had always sought out others to help define him. Dylan had chosen a postgraduate discipline because his father had suggested it. When that didn't work out, he followed in Leo's footsteps and undertook another career path. Dylan later took the job Leo had vacated, and he has been there ever since. So Dylan has always followed other people's directions and has never been able to figure out who he is and what he really wants to do. Because Dylan's parents, Leo, and then Dana, had always provided suggestions and guidance, their well-meaning efforts enabled Dylan to avoid making decisions on his own. His relationships were stymied as well. Dana eventually decided to take another job and move away because Dylan was unable to connect romantically with her. Their closeness had mimicked that of a twinship and had filled the void left by Leo's departure, but it never progressed beyond platonic friendship.

When I spoke with Dylan, we talked about how he might transition from the hopelessness he was feeling after the loss of his twin-like relationship to Dana to discovering what he really wants at this point in his life. He acknowledged that he wants fulfillment in his work and in his relationships, but that he needs to find out who he is as an individual apart from his brother and his family. I told him that while depending on his brother for many years certainly had an impact, the twinship may not have been wholly responsible for his ongoing sense of indecisiveness and uncertainty. Many factors determine a person's level of confidence and resolve. But it was clear that the twinship had inadvertently handicapped Dylan and kept him trapped in a state of not knowing who he was as an individual. By the time his brother left, Dylan's only option seemed to be finding another "twin."

Dylan's challenge is to overcome the handicap he has lived with for so long and to find a direction that feels authentically his. He agreed that seeing a therapist who understands twin-related dependency issues could help him with that transition.

"I Still Crave an Intense Relationship"—Ray's Story

When they were growing up, Ray and his twin brother Ramon always thought of themselves as individuals. They had different strengths, different friends, and, as Ray put it, they "didn't do that thing where we were at each other all the time." Still, the two were very close. They woke up at the same time together, went to school at the same time together, and even though they weren't in the same classes, they were almost always together. Like most twins, Ray took for granted the closeness he enjoyed with his brother. He didn't think their connection was anything out of the ordinary until he became an adult and began to notice how other relationships were not necessarily as intense or intimate. But he wanted that intimacy and believed he could recapture that intensity by marrying a twin. However, after five years they divorced. Ray admits that they did not really know one another before marrying because both assumed a twin-like intimacy not based upon their true selves. Nonetheless, he acknowledges that what he wants in a relationship is definitely tied to what he had as a twin. Ray explained:

> That's the weird thing. Now in my relationships, it is kind of odd that that's what I expect: a very committed relationship. My ex-wife is a twin, and I felt like we both understood that kind of bond that twins have, and it was really tight, a really close relationship with her as well. So that's kind of a path I sought.

His path was one that reflected the tight relationship he'd had with his twin brother, and certainly choosing another twin as his mate was one way to try to duplicate that close connection. Ray figured that since the woman he chose had also grown up as part of a twosome, she would know how to forge the type of tight bond within their marriage that she and Ray had each experienced as children with their respective twins. Although that did turn out to be the case, other problems in the marriage were unrelated to the couple's strong attachment or to their each being twins. Those problems could not be resolved, and the couple divorced. Now that Ray is seeing other women, he finds himself focusing on the level of intimacy he still yearns for, but which is not always easy to achieve.

> My ex-wife and I had a very close, almost intense relationship. And I think we were both comfortable with it because we were both twins. It is very interesting. I'm dating now, and it is not that I expect that, but it is something I'd like to have again. There is something comforting about having someone who is that close to you, and who you can trust that much. So, yeah, that is something I still crave. But do I think it's mandatory for my relationships? Not really. I think it is all going to come to pass, but now that I'm dating again I feel that I'm having those same struggles with the level of intimacy.

Ray and I talked about the expectation many twins have that intimacy will happen quickly and that an initial connection will lead to lasting rapport. Because twins don't have to work at being closely connected to each other, their experience is that closeness happens automatically. When they discover that this is not the case in the context of their other relationships, they can feel frustrated and dejected. Ray revealed that the relationship with his ex-wife began with an initial spark that ignited almost immediately. But he is now mature enough, and reflective enough, to realize that maintaining a strong relationship requires more than sparks.

> I'll tell you, with me and my ex-wife there was a very big initial spark. I've had one or two substantial relationships since, but I think intimacy takes a while to develop for most people. I think because I'm a twin, I'm more willing to open myself up to that possibility quicker than most people. So maybe it is true that that's something I'm longing for more.
>
> But as far as a marriage lasting, when I was younger I thought, "We're in love, we have this connection together, and all these other problems we can work out together." And I realize now that when you marry somebody you're not only marrying somebody you love, but this is somebody who you're going to be a partner with. This is your buddy, your teammate, the person you're going to rely on for a lot of other things, not just emotional security. So I've learned that it is more than just that initial spark.

Ray now understands that he doesn't have to get together with another twin in order to have a meaningful connection. And while he appreciates his twinship and acknowledges the high bar it set for him with regard to immediate intimacy, he is open to taking it more slowly with the women he is dating. If an initial spark fuels his interest in a potential new partner, he has learned to give himself time to consider the many facets of a couple's compatibility.

Avoiding a Twin-Like Friendship

Some twins may seek to replicate with a friend or lover what they had in their twinship, and then some want to avoid the dynamic they experienced with their twin. Some even go to the extreme of not making friends at all for fear they will be entrapped in another relationship that could threaten to undermine their hard-won individuality. Such was the case with thirty-three-year-old Maggie, who told me, "I don't have any friends because I don't want to need anyone. And I don't like needy people." While Maggie is very much a loner, her twin sister, Nadia, has a number of close friends and seems very comfortable in her attachments to people. Maggie, however, seems to sense that any attachment will be suffocating and intrusive. And she is not alone. Having struggled to establish their own identity after an overly close connection to their twin, such individuals worry that a close friendship means needing another person or being needed too much. So they prefer to be either on their own or to confine their social ties to casual acquaintances.

Yasmine, who was introduced in the last chapter, turned to her high school boyfriend for solace when her sister, Sophie, got sick. She soon found that the relationship with him became like another twinship. Although Yasmine wasn't aware of it at the time, she needed to continue the care-taking dynamic in which she had been immersed with her sister, and her boyfriend Will provided the other half of the equation. She leaned on him for moral support, and he counted on her to take care of him emotionally. They broke up after high school, and once she started college, Yasmine realized she had to break free from twin-like relationships if she was ever to discover who she was as an individual. This is how she explained it:

> My boyfriend was also my absolutely best friend. I did everything with him. I always felt like I was either Sophie's sister or Will's girl-friend—but I was never myself. I hate that I didn't know anything about myself. I depended on him for everything. It's almost scary how attached I got to Will. That's why I think I'm still not ready to be in a relationship because I still don't know who I am. I've figured out so much, but I don't feel like I've figured out enough.

I told Yasmine it is completely understandable that at eighteen she is still defining who she is. She had become like a twin with Will by using the only relationship she had had (her twinship) as a road map. And because both of those relationships had been codependent, neither had afforded her the opportunity to learn who she was as an individual apart from her twin or her boyfriend. I commended Yasmine for now taking the time to get to know herself, despite the pressure her parents seemed to be applying. She told me how they had reacted to her need to be on her own for a while:

Being on your own is so looked down upon, by society and by my parents . . . They go, "Why don't you have a boyfriend?" and I'm like, "Don't you understand, I'm just trying to figure myself out. I can't share myself with someone because I don't feel like I have as much as I could to share."

Yasmine told me she doesn't want to need someone again because she is finally becoming comfortable being with herself. She put it this way:

I never want that feeling of needing someone. Like recently I was needing this guy, and he would tell me every detail of his life. And I was thinking, "I don't want to tell you every detail of my life because I don't want to depend on you to tell me I have to get this or that done. I can deal with it by myself."

As Yasmine and I discussed her fear of getting involved with a boyfriend—or a close girlfriend—I told her that needing someone isn't necessarily a bad thing. Once you have gone through a process of defining yourself as an individual, and you feel secure in having your own identity, then you can be really clear about what your needs are. You won't need someone's support in order to feel confident, and you won't lose yourself in another person or give yourself over to meeting only their needs. Yasmine is presently engaged in this process but acknowledges that she has a ways to go. She wants to make friends without needing them in the way she once needed her twin sister. Her assessment of how much progress she has yet to make poignantly expressed the challenge she faces:

Sometimes I see people who are outgoing and I'll think, "How can they do this by themselves?" People will tell me, "You're really mature for your age," and yet I can't do something a second grader can do. I can't go and be a completely normal social person without Sophie.

Why do twins like Yasmine find it so difficult to be a "normal social person"? Because they grew up with a built-in buddy system and, like Yasmine, counted on their twin either to make the friends for them or didn't really need any other friends aside from their twin. So learning how to approach people without getting too close too soon or without losing oneself is very different than it is for singletons.

Yasmine is discovering that making friends doesn't have to mean finding another twin. And she's right. Second graders seem to make friends without even thinking about it. But they learn by trial and error. Some are better at it than others, and it takes practice.

"I'm kind of old to be so new at this," Yasmine said, "but it's time."

Replacing a Twin with a Best Friend

Sometimes twins form a best friendship after emotionally or physically separating from their same-age sibling, and doing so is not necessarily unhealthy. For twins, the template for friendship is their twinship, so it makes sense that some would want to continue to have a twin-like relationship with a best friend. The question becomes, are you gravitating toward a twin-like friendship because you are unable to navigate life on your own? Or is it simply a matter of enjoying the intensity of a close friendship? The stories that follow reveal that twin-like friendships can occur at any point in one's adult life.

In Carrie's case, it wasn't until she and her twin sister, Veronica, were in their early forties that Veronica found a best friend, leaving Carrie to nurse some very mixed feelings. Both sisters are married with teenage children. They had lived close to one another throughout their twenties and thirties, and Carrie had always taken her sister somewhat for granted.

Since they were only a ten-minute drive apart, they could always meet for coffee if they wanted to chat. More often though, they just picked up the phone or texted each other. They would also go out together about once a month with their husbands and the same group of mutual friends, so their social lives were closely connected as well. Then Veronica and her family moved to a town about four hours away. All of a sudden, the dynamics began to change between the sisters. Carrie described the nature of her relationship with Veronica prior to the move:

> We would telephone each other if there was a problem. And if something bothered her, I would know from the way she sent me a text message or from how she was on the phone. She would call me if something wasn't right, not for just a "la, la, la" ordinary conversation.

Carrie told me she still talks to Veronica on the phone, and their conversations are still mostly about whatever issue one of them is having with her kids, husband, or work. But it is the more intimate daily discussions that Carrie says she misses now. Veronica apparently has those kind of conversations with her new best friend. Carrie was very matter-of-fact as she began to explain that Veronica had made a friend with whom she now shared a big part of her life, a part Carrie has no access to. She paused a moment and then became teary while revealing that she felt envious of her sister's new friend:

> I just think I've got a jealous streak toward her friend. And it is an understandable jealous streak because whereas previously Veronica would have said to me, "Something's bothering me," now she says to her friend, "Something's bothering me." So we haven't really talked about it, but I can imagine that she's not going to be telling me things I'd like to hear because she's going to have that conversation with her friend.

It was obvious that Carrie felt very hurt and sad that Veronica seems closer to her new friend than she does to Carrie. But when I asked her if she might be able to express her feelings to Veronica without making

Veronica feel guilty (for example, "I'm happy for you that you have a new friend, but I feel kind of replaced"), Carrie said that would be impossible for her to do. She couldn't share those feelings with Veronica, she said, because she didn't want to prevent her from having a new friend. "For me to say to her that I feel hurt," Carrie explained, "it just wouldn't be fair to her because she's doing what she feels is right for her. And it wouldn't be fair for me to be selfish in that way."

Carrie's sensitivity with regard to how her sister might react shows that she cares deeply about Veronica and wants her to be able to have her own friends and her own life. It also demonstrates that Carrie believes such separation and independence from each other is essentially a good thing. But her sense of fairness and her belief that she and Veronica deserve to each go her own way do not mitigate her sadness. Carrie assumed she would always be Veronica's closest friend. Now, at the age of forty-something, she must adapt to the new reality of her sister's twin-like friendship.

The close friends that twin sisters Kim and Kara, now fifty-eight, made in college are still their best friends. Both concede that they forged twin-like best friendships almost immediately after the two separated. The sisters attribute the longevity of their respective friendships to their initial need for connections that mirrored their relationship to each other. Kara and Kim had been each other's only close friends during grade school and high school, but as they headed to different colleges and their lives went in different directions, they managed to find close girlfriends who would be as loyal and nurturing as their same-age sibling had been. The two had needed to stay closely connected to each other during their childhood because their mother was preoccupied with another child who had serious emotional problems. So the girls essentially mothered each other, although Kim assumed more of the caretaking role and Kara was the more withdrawn of the two. Once they were at separate colleges, the sisters missed the mutual support they had provided each other. So they gravitated to young women who could fill those supportive best friend roles. Kara told me:

I think that finding my girlfriend Marie, who is still my best friend, was like finding another Kim, another person who was outgoing and took me under her wing. I remember soon after we met she nicknamed me the "little lion" after the lion that lacks courage in *The Wizard of Oz*. I think Marie was my Kim.

Marie and Kara were roommates throughout college. Marie got Kara involved in a social circle on campus, and they did a lot of traveling together during summer breaks. Although the friends now live in separate cities, they talk on the phone several times a week, they travel together on occasion, and every year Kara makes a point to spend her birthday with Marie. When I asked her to describe what she finds appealing about her good friend, Kara told me that "Marie tends to be boisterous and somewhat domineering, but she laughs a lot and she's really very sweet. I have always been relatively shy and quiet, so I appreciate how she complements my personality." Kara admits that Marie complements her in essentially the same way that Kim used to—she's outgoing and takes charge. But whereas Kara eventually found Kim's dominant personality to be stifling and intrusive, Marie makes her feel comfortable in social situations. And Marie also makes her laugh. Kara continued:

> The fact that we're not sisters, we're not twins, we're just good friends—I don't get the same overwhelmed feeling I used to get with Kim. And I guess because I finally faced up to how uncomfortable I had always been with Kim being so overbearing around me, I know when to assert myself so it never gets to that point with Marie.

As for Kim, since she had been the caretaker when the sisters were growing up, it was not surprising she found as a best friend a young woman who also seemed to need caretaking. Kim, who has been in therapy and understands why she was drawn to someone like her friend Ellen, explained how their relationship began:

> I found a best friend I could kind of take care of, which is something I had always done. It sounds weird, but what I was attracted to most

about Ellen was that she was depressed. Her mother had just died, and she was feeling very vulnerable and down. I had no idea at the time that I was a caretaker or that I had been one as a twin, but I sensed she needed someone to kind of take care of her emotionally. And having lost my bearings when Kara and I separated, I needed someone I could do that for. So it was a match made in heaven.

Kim said she was often depressed in college, too, and Ellen was someone with whom she could share her emotions. She and Ellen weren't roommates, and they didn't socialize all the time, but when they did get together, their conversations were always "deep."

> I had other friends who were fun to be with, but superficial. My friendship with Ellen was deep. I could tell her how I was really feeling, about family problems, whatever. I told her all my deep, dark secrets, where I didn't tell those to my roommate—or to Kara. So it was that kind of a friendship. She was a safe person to share my depression with because she was depressed too.

Kim's depression stemmed in part from having grown up in a dysfunctional family in which she and Kara had to depend on one another for the nurturing their parents should have provided. Being a caretaker to Kara didn't fulfill that need, nor did being best friends with Ellen. But at least with Ellen, Kim was able to talk about her feelings and be herself; with Kara, she felt she had to be hypervigilant in order to attend to her sister's emotional needs.

After college, Kim and Ellen left for graduate school at different institutions and undertook careers in different cities, but they continued to visit each other as often as they could and kept in close touch by phone. Their ability to pour out their hearts to each other has never waned, and their conversations are as "deep" today as they were many years ago.

Kara and Kim are both married with children and have a number of other women friends, but their best friends play important roles in each of their lives. It is clear to the sisters that their twinship set the stage for the twin-like friendships they have maintained for over thirty years. Fortunately, they each have had the opportunity to reflect on their family history, their twinship prior to separating, and the emotional consequences of having been dependent on one another for so long. Although they chose best friends who had a lot in common with the other twin, they are aware of the danger in becoming too reliant on another person. They understand that a close friend, like a twin, can brighten and enrich your life, as long as you don't need that person in order to feel complete.

Assessing Your Twin-Like Relationship

How can you tell if the twin-like relationship you have with your best friend or significant other is psychologically healthy? Here are some guidelines to consider:

- Although you may miss your friend or significant other when he/she is not around, you don't require his/her presence in order to feel complete.

- Although you may value the emotional support your friend or significant other provides, you have a sense of your own inner strengths and resiliency and feel confident you can face challenges on your own.

- You enjoy the companionship of your friend or significant other but do not feel obligated to her/him or responsible for her/his well-being.

7

Conflicting Loyalties

I want my sister to be happy but she has had no empathy for what it is like for me, being single, being alone, not caring that I'm a third wheel.
                                                                                    —Lily, 34

My girlfriend doesn't know what she's getting into. If I had to choose, I am pretty sure I would always choose my brother, but how is it that she cannot be the most important one in my life? I am really scared about it.
                                                                                    —Ron, 31

Twins shouldn't have to be scared that a romantic attachment will jeopardize their twinship—but, like Ron, they often are. That is because most twins are tied to each other more closely than singleton siblings, and more intimately than best friends. When a best friend connects with a lover or decides to get married, the friend who is "left behind" may suffer temporarily but soon accepts one of life's fundamental realities: pairing off into a couple is what people do. In a twinship, such acceptance can be considerably more difficult and the suffering much more intense. If twins spend the first eighteen years or more of their lives as each other's partner and all of a sudden they're divested of that partnership, the shift in loyalties can be devastating.

In this chapter we'll explore how twinships are affected when one sibling becomes involved in a romantic relationship or gets married. As we'll discover, the degree to which twins confront conflicting loyalties depends on their level of connectedness. The spectrum ranges from twins who are close but individuated to those who essentially function as a couple—with various gradations in between. It can be particularly challenging for someone whose twin has always been one's primary relationship to begin to consider a boyfriend, girlfriend, or spouse as the most important person in his life. And it is not uncommon for the unattached twin to react like a jilted lover, even if he acknowledges that it is unhealthy to cling to one's adult sibling.

Added to the mix is the relationship between the significant other and the unattached twin, who may both be vying for the attached twin's undivided attention. Some partners accept the fact that being involved with a twin means sharing her or him with another devoted companion. Others find themselves embroiled in ongoing conflicts over who takes priority: one's twin or one's mate.

Jealousy, loneliness, and a sense of loss often plague the twin who is forced to give up twin togetherness. And for the newly attached twin the challenge is not only to cope with the guilt over abandoning one's sibling but learning to feel entitled to an intimate relationship. For both twins, adapting to changes in the twinship may be difficult or even traumatic but can ultimately lead to profound personal growth.

Sorting Out the Issues

A number of statements in my Adult Twin Survey specifically address the issues related to conflicting loyalties. These statements represent a range of concerns including doubts about forging a relationship that is as close as one's twinship, worry that one's twin will feel abandoned, and envy over a twin's romantic involvement. Respondents whose stories appear in this chapter answered yes to several of the following statements:

- I can't imagine loving anyone as much as my twin—and that worries me.

- My boyfriend/girlfriend/spouse resents how close I am with my twin, and I don't know what to do about it.

- I feel ashamed that I don't want my twin to feel closer to his/her partner than he/she feels toward me.

- It bothers me that my twin doesn't approve of my choice in partners, and I worry that I'm too influenced by his/her opinions.

- I think my relationship with my boyfriend/girlfriend/spouse would be much better if I didn't have to worry about my twin.

It would be extremely rare for singleton siblings to have such worries, but for twins these issues can be troubling indeed. Many survey respondents offered further comments that elucidated their concerns, a few of which appear below. When I read these statements, I was struck by how agonizing it can be for twins to enter into an intimate relationship when they are enmeshed with or overly close to their same-age sibling.

- "It is challenging for me to accept another person as an adequate life partner."—37-year-old male

- "I can't admit it in front of her, because I don't want her to think she has become less important to me. It's just that someone else, probably my future husband, has entered into my life and he has become as important to me."—18-year-old female

- "The closeness I feel with my spouse does not compare to the closeness I feel toward my twin. I could live without him; I doubt I could live long or well without my twin."—58-year-old female

- "I wonder how a man will feel when he starts to date me and realizes I have a relationship with my sister that he won't be able to understand but has to accept."—32-year-old female

British psychotherapist and renowned twin specialist Audrey C. Sandbank concurs that twins may face a number of obstacles when they enter into romantic relationships. She refers to the hesitancy some twins have about forming a new partnership, the fear of being disloyal to one's twin, and the worry that no partner can take the place of one's twin. "Twins, who for many years have lived with someone who understood their moods and feelings and who may have intuitively known what they were thinking or what they would like to do, may feel disappointed and cheated if their new partner fails to live up to such standards."[9]

Such feelings of disappointment are certainly evident in the fifty-eight-year-old female respondent's remarks above. After years of marriage, she has determined that her husband is a lesser priority in her life than her twin, even going so far as to state that she could live without him but not without her twin.

The sense that one cannot live happily unless the twinship continues to be one's primary relationship is a theme that runs through a number of twins' stories. Those who feel this way are nearly always the ones who never had the chance to separate from their twin in childhood and therefore are unable to function emotionally without their same-age sibling partnership. Lily's story reflects such circumstances.

"I'm Adjusting to the Fact That She Will *Always* Put Him before Me"—Lily's Story

In her midthirties, Lily is struggling to get used to her twin sister Darlene's married status. It is not as if the two sisters had been exclusive partners as adults; Lily had been seriously involved with someone for six years. But when that relationship broke up, she expected that her close ties to her twin would sustain her. Underlying emotional issues surfaced, however, during the months leading up to her sister's wedding. Lily explained:

> Planning Darlene's wedding was one of the worst times for us. I was
> still adjusting to being single. She was planning a wedding and acting

entitled to have everything go her way. It was as if getting married gave her an excuse to have everything revolve around her.

Although most people cut some slack for a bride-to-be who is understandably entitled to be the center of attention prior to her wedding, Lily concluded that her sister's behavior was extremely selfish. The emotional turmoil calmed down somewhat after the wedding, but Lily is still challenged by the shift in her relationship with Darlene. Finding herself the odd woman out among her married friends—and now her married sister—Lily continues to look to Darlene to fill in the empty spaces in her life:

> At times I tend to depend on Darlene to entertain me, as most of our friends are married with children and do not socialize the way we used to. Being single I don't really have anyone to count on to do things with me, and at times I try to get her to do what I want.

Even if Lily were not a twin, being the only single woman in a group of friends who are all married would still be tough. Having grown up with a quasi partner whom she could always count on for companionship makes the current situation even more challenging. I think Lily not only resents her sister's lack of sufficient attention and concern, she also dislikes her own neediness. Frustrated by her single status, she acknowledges that her history as a twin has left her unprepared to adequately cope with her sister's marriage. "It can get frustrating being alone," she said, "especially for someone who never has been their entire life." Interestingly, Lily seems to characterize Darlene's alleged clinginess to her new husband in a way that actually reflects Lily's yearning to regain the coupled relationship she and her sister once shared:

> In a way I believe Darlene has kind of replaced the relationship she always tried to get from me with him. If you speak to her, she will tell you they do things separately; but it is a joke between a few of our friends that she won't do anything without him, and wants him invited to everything, and even complains at times when we try to plan a girls' thing.

Lily is clearly suffering. She is jealous of the closeness between the newlyweds and feels hurt by what she perceives as her sister's selfishness. From Lily's perspective, Darlene is thinking only about herself and not about Lily.

Lily is not alone in castigating her twin sister as selfish for loosening the ties that once bound them together. This raises a crucial issue. It is important to consider the concept of selfishness as it applies to twins who are shifting their primary loyalty from sibling to mate. The contention of many unattached twins who suffer when their same-age sibling finds a mate is that their twin is thinking only of what will please them, and not the twin who has been "abandoned." I tell my clients who are in this situation that selfishness has a distinctly positive connotation when it applies to twins acting in their own best interest after a lifetime of tending to their sibling's emotional needs. Lily has cast Darlene as the selfish one for wanting to spend so much time with her husband and for lacking empathy by dismissing Lily's complaints of abandonment. But being selfish in this way is actually a very healthy sign; it signals that Darlene is learning to set boundaries that should have been established earlier.

By relinquishing the obligation to constantly worry about the other twin's feelings, a twin can begin to navigate the perfectly normal path toward living her own life. On the other hand, if the attached twin continues to be preoccupied with the unattached twin feeling left out, she can get pulled back into the dysfunctional marriage of twinship—rather than developing a healthy relationship or marriage with the partner she's chosen. And tending to the emotional needs of an adult sibling will not benefit that individual in her quest to find a meaningful relationship of her own.

In further conversations with Lily, I learned she is still struggling with all the old conflicts revolving around her twinship: feeling that she has always had to make sacrifices for Darlene, feeling angry about making those sacrifices, wanting Darlene's undivided attention but then feeling guilty for wanting it, and wanting to have her own identity but feeling stuck in her attempt to define herself. I think that as it becomes clear to Lily that her history with Darlene has made it difficult for her to adjust to Darlene's marriage and the new dynamic between them, she will be able to shift her focus from Darlene's alleged selfishness to her own current needs.

Lily would like to be in a relationship herself, but she doesn't want to be involved with anyone who is too needy for fear of replicating a codependent, twin-like dynamic. I have heard other twins express this concern as well. Although they don't want to be with someone who will lean on them too heavily, that is the type of person whom they always seem to attract. I tell these individuals, as I told Lily, that their challenge is to get in touch with their own needs and to make sure that those needs are met when they become involved in a serious relationship. As simple as that may sound, I think many twins who have been in a codependent relationship with their same-age sibling experience a lot of uncertainty when it comes to answering these questions: What are my needs in a relationship? Is this person satisfying those needs? To what degree can I allow myself to be needed? And does this person's neediness go beyond the threshold at which I feel comfortable? For Lily, the conundrum continues to be confusing. But she realizes that a lifetime of being a twin has contributed to her confusion, and she is committed to discovering who she is as an individual and what she wants from a relationship.

"Why Would My Sister-in-Law Drive a Wedge between Two Brothers?"—Bruce's Story

Bruce and Barry grew up lacking the necessary attention and nurturing from their parents, who divorced when the boys were seven. Their mother remarried when the twins were twelve, and although their stepfather is a nice person, neither he, the biological dad, nor the mom was very involved with the children. As is often the case in such circumstances, the boys turned to each other. "We were each other's father and mother," Bruce said.

Being together was all-important. Bruce remembers one summer when they were ten; he and Barry went to different summer camps, and the separation clearly had an effect on Bruce. "When Barry came home from his camp, he seemed like a different person, and it scared me. But a few days later he was back to his old self." It seems the brief time away from each other, engaging in different activities and meeting different people, felt threatening and scary to ten-year-old Bruce.

In high school, Bruce stopped liking his twin status. He says he "felt like a freak" and wanted Barry to walk five paces behind him so they didn't have to appear together. Bruce would even change his posture if he saw Barry sitting the same way. They had many physical fights during that time, with just one rule: no blows to the head.

After high school they went to separate colleges. Bruce says he loved his college experience and made lifelong friends. A traumatic event occurred during this time, however. Bruce fell in love with a woman who was killed in a car accident. He says that Barry sent him letters expressing his love and support, which were very meaningful to him at the time and which Bruce continues to reflect upon as a testament to the brothers' closeness.

When the brothers were in their late twenties, Barry got engaged. It didn't work out, but Bruce remembers how he reacted at the time: "I panicked. I thought, 'I have to get married, too!'" Such a reaction is common among twins who have not developed a strong enough sense of self. The need to be the same as and equal to one's twin may extend to the need to equalize one's marital status.

Barry eventually got married, and at that time Bruce was still single. Barry made it clear to Bruce that he couldn't talk to him on the phone as often and that Bruce shouldn't be as dependent upon him anymore. According to Bruce, Barry shut him out of his life for almost six months. Bruce was very angry and did not understand why his brother would turn from him so callously. Barry's wife was apparently very threatened by the brothers' closeness and accused her brother-in-law of being overly dependent on her husband. "She resents that my brother and I have an intimate relationship," Bruce told me. "Why would my sister-in-law drive a wedge between two brothers? Why can't she understand that we have a different kind of affection for each other?"

I tried to explain to Bruce that perhaps he was not being considerate enough of Barry's need to have his own life. Bruce admitted that he was irate when Barry told him that he needed his space. "I disagreed with what he was trying to tell me," Bruce said. "I even called him an idiot, and then Barry got angry and threatened not to talk to me anymore. He gave me an ultimatum, just like his wife gives him."

As we discussed the combative dynamic that had developed between him and his brother, Bruce acknowledged he was still relating to Barry as a single twin brother, without regard for Barry's new relationship and his desire and need for separateness. It was as if the two were back in high school; only now they were going at it with heated words rather than clenched fists. As teenagers, they had begun to feel the need to develop separate identities, and the fear and anger accompanying that need brought on numerous clashes. With Barry's decision to pull away from Bruce so that he could focus more intently on his wife, the brothers' separateness once again sparked fear and anger in Bruce.

Bruce agreed with this explanation. As difficult as it was for him to create new boundaries between himself and his twin, he understood how important it was to accept Barry's wish for increased autonomy.

Bruce is now married and better understands how one's marriage becomes a priority, and rightfully so. Still, he is upset that Barry continues to keep their contact to a minimum. They live in separate cities and have made plans to get together only to have them cancelled at the last minute, due to unilateral decisions by Barry's wife.

> We didn't talk for a long time after that last disappointment because I was so mad at him for canceling this trip. I felt like he was being really spineless, letting his wife pressure him. He just said, "Well, Bruce, this

is what I have to do—you can understand" and he wasn't apologetic
about it, so I was very pissed.

Bruce is sad and disappointed that his relationship with his brother
is not nearly as intimate as it was before Barry was married. He says that
while he understands that is what happens when people get married and
have families, he disagrees with Barry's position. Bruce says that his own
wife has no problem with the brothers getting together, and he resents the
fact that Barry's wife does everything she can to thwart Bruce's contact
not only with Barry but also with their parents. "I feel that you can have
a primary family and still have a close relationship with your parents and
a close relationship with your siblings," Bruce said. "It doesn't have to be
one or the other. I think there are ways to balance that."

But apparently Barry is unable to have a relationship with Bruce because
his wife demands his exclusive loyalty. And because Barry is threatened by
the possibility of his wife leaving him if he opposes her demands, he sticks
with the status quo even though it means having little time with his brother.

As for why his sister-in-law might be "driving a wedge" between the
brothers, I explained to Bruce that certain insecure individuals cannot allow
their spouse to have another intimate relationship—be it with a friend, a
singleton sibling, or a twin—because they perceive it as a serious threat.
And a twinship can be especially threatening to a spouse who requires
constant attention, devotion, and validation. Unfortunately, Barry is not
capable of talking to Bruce about any of his feelings, which are likely quite
conflicted concerning his wife and his twin brother. He can only state
that his wife won't let him do such and such—and rationalize his decision to go along with her pronouncements by declaring that Bruce is too
dependent on him.

Bruce can't do much to alter the current stalemate. He feels the loss
of his brother's companionship and resents Barry's wife's controlling
nature. But Bruce recognizes that it is Barry's choice to stand up to his
wife—or not.

"My Husband Has Had to Endure Our Twenty-Five-Year Marriage with an Extra Person"—Rhonda's Story

When I asked Rhonda to describe her relationship to her twin sister, Tracy, she revealed the degree to which their lives are joined and the mixed blessing that has resulted from their unusually close connection.

> My sister and I are going to be fifty next month. And we have been together forever, including my twenty-five-year marriage. Tracy never married and she lives down the street. So she has pretty much helped me raise my four kids. She is like a second mother to my children, and it has been so wonderful. I mean, I've been really lucky. She dated a little bit, but nothing ever worked out.

While Rhonda feels lucky to have had a second mom for her children and a close companion whom she can always count on, her good fortune is mitigated by the fact that her sister's brief relationships have never worked out. She hinted that Tracy's single status might be due in part to their twin-ship, but prefaced that remark with her contention that Tracy has been happy in her supportive role:

> She's been happy to accommodate me. She was the wind beneath my wings. And still is. I still hold out hope that maybe she will meet someone, but she's always been very happy to be with me. I've read that oftentimes twins will not get married because they have already found a perfect relationship and they're very content in the relation-ship that they've had with their twin. I know that my sister and I will be close until the day one of us leaves this earth.

According to Rhonda, the arrangement she and Tracy have had for the last twenty-five years has worked out well for both of them. Although her sister never got married or had children, Rhonda says Tracy has enjoyed being closely attached to her nieces and nephews and seamlessly integrated into Rhonda's family. And Rhonda has been happy to provide that experi-ence: "Tracy wasn't as lucky as I to meet someone and have children of her own. I didn't want her to never have that experience, so I was happy to share it with her."

As for Rhonda's husband, Mel, Rhonda says he has accepted Tracy as part of their family, even though "it has been hard for him at times." When I asked how Mel has felt all these years about Rhonda including her sister in their day-to-day family life, Rhonda explained:

> Mel actually worked with Tracy when they were younger, and that's how I met him. We were bowling one night, and he was there, and she introduced us. So they knew each other before I met him. And he knew how close we were. So it was like a natural progression that when we moved to this neighborhood, she moved here too.
>
> But I think it has been hard on my husband because my relationship with my sister—I don't want to say it's a perfect relation-ship—but I think that when you've always had somebody there, you don't need your spouse a hundred percent of the time.
>
> My husband has been so wonderful and let it happen even though it has been hard for him at times. There've been times when we've had some rough patches and maybe he thought if she wasn't in the picture I would be there more for him.

During the course of our interview, when Rhonda mentioned that "it has been hard" on her husband or that "at times it's been a problem" for him that her sister plays such a prominent role in their family, she failed to fully elaborate; instead, she often changed the subject. It seemed as if it was a topic she may have been avoiding. I asked more pointedly how Mel felt about Tracy being a second mom to his children, and about Rhonda needing him less due to her intimate ties with her sister. At first Rhonda responded by saying that "maybe credit should be given to my husband for being such a really giving, wonderful person and unselfish in that way." But then she went on to tell me that, after withholding his feelings for years, Mel finally expressed his resentment in a "blowup" argument:

> He sort of held it all in, and then it finally culminated in a blowup, which just crushed my sister—because I don't think she had ever

heard anything like that from him. He didn't address it straight to her, but we had a big blowup in front of her and he said things like "Your sister is always here and that's why the kids are behaving the way they are—they know that even if we say no, they can always get their way with their Aunt Tracy!"

After the quarrel, Tracy told Rhonda she was not going to come over anymore. Rhonda was very upset and angry at her husband. "I was angry because he crushed her," Rhonda said, "and Tracy did not deserve to be crushed." When I asked Rhonda what she meant by the word "crushed" she said Mel had badly hurt Tracy's feelings.

Mel called Tracy and apologized for his outburst, and after a few weeks of Rhonda pleading with Tracy to spend time at their house again, Tracy agreed—but only on the weekends. The fact was that Mel did not want Tracy there every day, and Tracy understood that. Rhonda said, "I think she knows that it's only fair to him, as my husband, that he have some time alone with his family."

It wasn't until Mel took a stand that the sisters realized a change was in order. Rhonda and her husband needed more time together, and Tracy's prominent role in Rhonda's immediate family needed to be downsized. Rhonda admits, however, that she could never have been the one to establish those ground rules. "Of course I could understand that Mel didn't want Tracy here every day," Rhonda told me. "And I know that's right. But I would not have crushed my own sister like that. I didn't have it in me to do that."

While sharing his family with Tracy has been a struggle for Mel, it has been a comfort and a joy for Rhonda. She is worried about what the future holds, though. Rhonda said she is concerned about how the family dynamic and her twinship will change once her children go to college.

> I worry about the time when my children are all grown and my husband wants to spend more alone time with me. I worry about Tracy because there are obviously going to be times when it will be just me and my husband, and rightfully so. And I would like for her to meet someone and have that experience and find happiness with

someone else. But I think that we're just so used to each other and so content in our relationship that it has been really hard for her. I think that on a Saturday night she'd rather spend it with me than potentially go out with someone who she is probably not going to like anyway.

When I asked Rhonda about the chances of Tracy eventually meeting someone and having a relationship of her own, Rhonda responded as the dominant twin she has always been by saying, "Maybe I'm going to have to give her the push to do something she wouldn't necessarily do on her own—maybe it's coming to that time."

"I Miss Him More Than I Can Tell My Wife"—Scott's Story

Throughout their thirty-three years, Scott and his brother, Lyle, have had their ups and downs, their periods of having fun together and their struggles to break away from each other. As Scott put it, "We have abandoned each other all of our lives and then come back."

As young boys, they were inseparable. Scott said that early on he was essentially placed in the role of Lyle's caretaker by their parents, who still affectionately refer to Lyle as "baby." Part of Scott's caretaking role involved making sure he never surpassed Lyle in any way. Scott said he deliberately monitored himself in schoolwork, sports, even video games, so that his brother would never feel inferior. "If we were playing a video game and Lyle was losing, he would throw down the controller—so I made sure that didn't happen."

Scott describes Lyle as immature, overly emotional, and someone who needs lots of attention. On the other hand, sometimes Scott depended on Lyle socially because Lyle was the more outgoing twin. Scott told me that in junior high, "I was awkward and isolated, and Lyle was sociable. He let me be with his friends, and I hung on to him and his friends." The brothers' closeness was further strengthened by their common interest in gymnastics. "When we were fourteen, we bonded together through our commitment to gymnastics," Scott said, "and we had a healthy competition. Sometimes I won and other times he won."

In high school the brothers began to go their separate ways, with Lyle being more adamant about wanting his space. "He was embarrassed by me, as I did not conform," Scott said. But when they got to college, the pendulum swung in the other direction. This time it was Scott who was more in touch with his need for more separation. Still, the push-pull dynamic of fighting for his need to separate from Lyle and then returning to the comfort of their twinship existed.

> In college we joined different fraternities, but when his fraternity folded, he wanted to be with me—and sometimes I just could not stand it. Our relationship began to get really strained when we became roommates. He and I had different social priorities and often fought, physically sometimes. But we always worked things out and generally enjoyed each other's company.

Scott says he and Lyle now have a good relationship. After college, they moved to the same city but grew apart due to their demanding careers. There are also issues with Scott's wife. She prefers not to socialize with Scott's side of the family and avoids events involving his relatives. Although she tells Scott he is free to see his family, her position has resulted in Scott getting together with Lyle much less frequently than he would like.

While they don't have a chance to see each other often, Scott says that when he and Lyle do get together it is always fun, and if a disagreement or conflict arises, they are both forgiving. They appreciate the occasions when they are together, perhaps because they are so infrequent. But Scott confesses that he misses his brother.

> I enjoy the autonomy that I have been able to develop in my adult years, but I do miss my brother sometimes. Our wives and families have become our new priorities, and we do not have the time to give one another like we once did. I see him once a month or so, but wish it was more.

It seems that Scott's wife has forced the issue of marital versus sibling loyalty and has laid down the law that their marriage should always take precedence. Scott says that because she was an only child, his wife doesn't understand how close the brothers have always been and how much they enjoy each other's company. But he doesn't want to rock the boat by challenging her.

> I miss him more than I can tell my wife, who is an only child and doesn't understand the bond we have. I wish I could spend more time with my brother, but I feel conflicted considering more time with him would mean less time with my wife . . . so I don't do anything about it.

Scott justifies his wife not spending time with his relatives by saying, "that is how she grew up." He adds, however, that she *does* make time for her own family. Perhaps Scott's wife's avoidance of his family's get-togethers has less to do with her upbringing and more to do with her competitiveness with Lyle. While Scott suppresses his feelings of missing his brother, his wife is likely well aware of the brothers' deep connection. She may not be privy to such statements as those Scott shared with me below, but she most likely senses the emotions underlying them.

> My brother and I have an instant bond and camaraderie. Years can go by and it happens right up again, just because of our boyhood connection. We'll relate to each other just like in junior high. We have always been ships passing in the night, but when we collide we do so because it's nice—and fun.

Did Scott choose as a mate someone who would make sure that he kept a certain distance from his brother, even though he still misses Lyle? I get the sense that Scott wants to do the right thing by having his wife as his priority; yet, if it were up to him, he might spend more time with his brother. In fact, I think Scott is ambivalent. He is most likely using his wife's unwillingness to be with his family as a way to avoid them as well. He is so conflicted about being close to his brother and his family that he claims he can't be involved because his wife doesn't want to be. I think this may be a way for Scott to avoid resolving his conflicts with his brother and his family. Instead of figuring out how to deal with the situation in a way that addresses his own needs, Scott uses his wife as an excuse so that he can postpone making his own decisions.

Meanwhile, he still misses his brother.

"My Husband Didn't Realize When He Married Me That He Kind of Married Two People"—Chloe's Story

When he and Chloe were first married, Chloe's husband, Ted, didn't have any qualms about their buying a duplex with Chloe's twin sister, Miranda (whose story is in chapter 5). He was in his late twenties, the sisters were a few years older, and it seemed like a reasonable solution to the first-time homebuyer challenge. The three had lived together briefly with no problems, and since Miranda was in a graduate program in another city, she would be around only on weekends. Ted was well aware that his wife and her sister were close, but he didn't yet know the extent to which the women's lives would continue to be intimately connected. Chloe explains:

> Ted's the one who suggested that we buy a duplex together. And I just think he had no idea what it was going to be like to be married to a twin. He figured he had lived with us for a few months, so of course it would all work out. She would have her place, we would have ours. But after the first few months of living together, he looked at me and said, "Can you at least tell her to knock before she comes in?" And I hadn't even thought about it. I was like, "Really? Oh, okay."

Even more troubling for Ted than the unacknowledged open-door policy was the emotional impact Miranda's problems had on Chloe. The sisters had been empathic toward one another throughout their lives, and Chloe's married status didn't change that ingrained dynamic.

> I loved having her live upstairs, but at the same time it was hard because if things were going badly for her, it trickled down. I was that much more aware of what was going on in her life, and I couldn't

remove myself. It is very hard to be happy when your twin is frantic, or intensely depressed, or really upset about something—and you just can't get past it as the other twin. And I know that my husband found that very frustrating.

Perhaps one of the most contentious issues Ted and Chloe have faced in their fourteen years of marriage is the question of moving to the opposite side of the country, where Ted has been offered important career opportunities and where Chloe has always claimed she wanted to relocate. But once she started seriously considering the move, the thought of living thousands of miles from her sister seemed so painful that Chloe wasn't sure she could do it.

> For a very long time I had wanted to move back east. And there was a point when my husband got what could have been a very lucrative job offer, which thank God, didn't work out. And I remember being on the phone with Miranda and our best friend, having a conference call, and talking about the move. I was hyperventilating. I could not deal with the fact of moving that far away from her. It was just overwhelming. I've lived on my own before, and I moved to Europe by myself, but those experiences didn't feel permanent. This would have been.

When I asked her to describe the panic she felt when she considered living that far away from her sister, Chloe told me that just knowing she could be with Miranda any time she wanted is a tremendous comfort, and she was afraid to give that up.

> We might not see each other all week, we'll talk once or twice or sometimes not at all during the day, but I always know that I can see her. It's an option. She's there. And there have only been a few years out of our lives when she wasn't. But my lack of desire to move back east caused a lot of problems in my marriage.

Chloe knows that her reticence about moving contributed to Ted's sense that Miranda was his wife's first priority. In fact, Chloe dreaded having to choose between her husband and her sister, so when Ted decided not to move she was very relieved. "Choosing between them would be a tight race," she said. "I don't think I'd ever say it to Ted's face, but it would have been a tight race. It is hard because there's an ease and a comfort with Miranda that I don't think I could ever have with anybody else."

Unlike many other twins in this book, Chloe and Miranda were brought up to value their separate identities. Chloe says both of her parents treated the sisters as individuals, didn't dress them alike, and never referred to them as "the twins." Whenever possible, they made sure the girls were placed in separate classes. Still, Chloe believes that the close connection between twins is inevitable. "I think it comes with the territory," she says. "There's so much angst around being a twin, but there's never any doubt that that love is there. It is just a given."

So how has Ted adjusted to being married to a twin after all these years? According to Chloe, the twinship has actually provided him with certain benefits that Ted has learned to appreciate.

> In the beginning of our relationship, Ted was jealous of my bond with Miranda. But he grew to understand that I didn't love her more, just differently. Gradually he understood that she's a valuable part of my life, someone who I can chat endlessly with when he can't stand to say another word! Sometimes he sees it as a relief because he doesn't always have to be the one to listen to me. There's this other person that I can go talk to.

Still, the issue of conflicting loyalties will surface, sometimes in an unexpectedly mundane context. Chloe explains:

> We've been married now for fourteen years, and we've been together sixteen. But it's still hard for him. Like I had a screensaver on my computer, and it was of me and Miranda and our kids—on a day when our two families went to the beach. And Ted said, "Yeah, of course you like this picture of you and your sister" and I went, "Just as often I have a picture of us as a family!" It was odd to me that he would make a comment like that, even after all these years.

Spouses and Twins

It is not unusual for spouses like Ted to feel that they are competing with a wife's (or husband's) twin. Being married to a twin presents distinct challenges, one of which is coping with feelings of jealousy and competitiveness. Spouses who tend to feel the least jealous or competitive are those who are the most secure within themselves and therefore enjoy the most secure attachment to their husband or wife. Knowing that their marriage is strong, they are generally not threatened by their mate having a close relationship to his or her twin. They are able to recognize and appreciate the value of their spouse's attachment to the twin, and are pleased the twin can provide a special sensitivity for their spouse that they cannot.

With that said, it is incumbent upon a twin to educate her or his spouse about the nature of twinship, what it has meant in her or his life, and the importance it continues to have. It is also crucial for the twin to make her marriage a priority. I have heard many twins talk about their twinship as their "first marriage," an unbreakable bond that is impossible for any future relationship to match. But allowing your actual marriage to take precedence does not mean you must break the bond with your twin. It means that you give yourself the time and energy to enjoy the relationship with your spouse and that you afford yourselves the privacy every marriage deserves. Worrying that your twin will feel left out or hurt if you spend however much time you want to spend with your spouse is not healthy for you, your twin, or your marriage.

Guidelines for Dealing with Conflicting Loyalties

You might find it challenging to figure out how to make room for significant relationships in your life without alienating your twin. The following suggestions can facilitate a healthier transition.

- Educate your significant other about your twin relationship and the challenges you face in dealing with twin-related issues.

- Avoid comparing your marriage (or other primary relationship) with the twinship. Make sure your expectations pertain to a significant other, not your same-age sibling.

- Give your marriage (or your relationship) the attention it deserves. Realize that feeling guilty for having a significant other and allegedly abandoning your twin is understandable but unhealthy.

- Be aware that your significant other won't necessarily have a close relationship with your twin. It is great if everyone gets along, but don't expect your twin to adore your choice in partners or your partner to appreciate your twin as much as you do.

- Be aware of negative or hostile comments your twin might make regarding your significant other. You can listen to your twin's feelings without allowing them to threaten your marriage or relationship.

- Be open with your spouse or partner about conflicts/issues between the two of you. Develop healthy means of communication and problem solving.

8

Claiming Your Self

Heading in separate directions was kind of organic. We were both athletic, but after school I'd go do my thing and he'd go do his thing, so we had these separate groups—but there was also a lot of commonality outside of those groups . . . Today, even though we hold very different and strongly felt opinions, it doesn't seem to be a big deal. Our friendship is unassailable.   —Drew, 50

When I go to work, I am ME. People are aware that I have a twin sister and they've met her. But they don't know her. And I do like that I can have my own identity, that there's no comparison made.
                                                            —Alicia, 58

Alicia's willingness to confront her twin comparison issues resulted in a life-changing transition: she became motivated to discover who she wanted to be as an individual. Drew did not have to make that transition because he had always experienced a healthy separateness from his twin brother. Both Drew and Alicia embody a strong sense of self while also enjoying close and rewarding relationships with their same-age siblings.

In this final chapter, we'll explore how you can claim your individuality and uniqueness, even though you may be dealing with some of the twin-related issues highlighted throughout the book. Perhaps you never considered these dilemmas prior to reading about them here. Or maybe you were concerned about codependency, separation anxiety, caretaking, competition, or conflicting loyalties within your twinship but felt guilty or worried about acknowledging your concerns. After reading the stories in the preceding chapters, you now know that you are not alone, that a lot of twins face very similar problems, and that acknowledging them won't put your twinship at risk. To the contrary, you and your twin will be able to relate to each other in a more authentic, meaningful way when you have a clearer perspective on your relationship.

Most adult twins feel fortunate to have a sibling with whom they share a family history and an ongoing companionship. But you are also entitled to your own identity, a sense of yourself as a stand-alone individual. In this chapter we'll address the questions that adult twins most often grapple with as they go through the process of claiming their individuality, including:

- How do I begin to explore who I am and what I want, apart from my twin?

- Must I physically separate from my twin in order to resolve dependency issues?

- How can I communicate to my twin that I want to change aspects of our relationship without hurting her/his feelings?

In the following pages you'll discover answers to these questions. We'll hear from Alicia and Drew, and we'll also recap key stories of adult twins who enjoy a strong relationship with their sibling while maintaining the separateness that allows them to thrive as individuals. As you reflect on how these twins achieved their sense of individuality, I believe you will be inspired to begin (or continue) the process of claiming your distinct self, which is every person's birthright.

"I Hold My Head High"—Alicia's Story

Alicia and her sister, Cheryl, lead very different lives, but at fifty-eight, they still compare themselves to each other. In our interview, Alicia jokingly mentioned that Cheryl wondered why I didn't want to interview her since they had both filled out the Adult Twin Survey. (I did want to interview Cheryl; I just hadn't scheduled the interview yet.) Cheryl had asked Alicia, "Why do you think she doesn't want to talk to me?" and Alicia replied teasingly, "I don't know, Cheryl, maybe I answered my questions better than you did!" Alicia said they laughed about the friendly competitive streak that runs through their ultraclose relationship. Cheryl is married to someone who earns a very comfortable living, so she has never had to work outside the home. Alicia and her husband are both employed but don't earn the amount of income to do what Cheryl's family does, such as taking expensive vacations or sending their children to pricey summer camps. Several decades ago, Alicia's tendency to measure her status and achievements against her twin sister's came to a head during a fitness class to which Cheryl had invited her. Alicia heard Cheryl talking with friends about shopping at exclusive boutiques, planning European trips, and dining at chic restaurants. Comparing her twin's easy life to her own economic struggles was a hard pill to swallow, as Alicia explained:

> I went home crying. It really brought it to the forefront how different our lives were. And I remember that day our washing machine broke and I had gone to the class worrying about "How are we going to afford another washing machine?" And here she was just having a good time with her exercise group discussing their next posh vacation.

Alicia admits she was envious of Cheryl. "I'll be honest," she told me, "I wanted the ease of her life." But rather than continue to be miserable comparing her lifestyle to her sister's, Alicia decided to do something for herself that would not only improve her economic situation but take her life in a new direction. She resolved to go back to school and get her teaching credential.

> I realized I don't have the money to do the things she did with her children, and I have never articulated this to Cheryl, but it did bother me tremendously that I could not. And there was a time when I kind of pulled away from her for a while. But what really helped me was to go back to school and get my own identity—something that I could take pride in for myself.

Interestingly, Cheryl reacted to Alicia's new undertaking by comparing her own lack of education to Alicia's professional achievement. She was supportive of Alicia but began questioning her own life choices. And even as Alicia told me how Cheryl had compared her nonacademic background to Alicia's newly minted teaching credential, she brought up Cheryl's superior culinary skills, yet another example of the continued focus on comparing her life to her twin's:

> Cheryl was very helpful and supportive when I went back to school, as was my husband—extremely so. And I do know she respects me for what I did, so I hold my head high about that. And sometimes she'll say to me, "Alicia, it bothers me that I have not pursued a further education" and I say to her, "but you've been educated with other things"—she's traveled, she studied art, she is a gourmet cook and can pull off a meal that you wouldn't believe. I remember one time my son said to me after they'd been at Cheryl's, "Aunt Cheryl never makes anything out of a can!" (Alicia laughs.) Here I'm trying to work and hold a family together, and Cheryl's feeding them these from-scratch meals!

Cheryl told me she was obviously aware of the economic differences between her family and Alicia's, and that she sometimes worried about having been insensitive. For example, she remembered discussing with Alicia that she and her husband were moving because they needed a larger home, without being sensitive to the fact that Alicia could not even afford the "smaller" house they were moving out of. But in drawing the comparison between her and Alicia's relationship to money, Cheryl admitted she is under certain financial constraints that Alicia isn't; that is, Cheryl doesn't "hold the purse strings" in her family. Cheryl explained:

> As secure as we are, I don't have the same access to money that Alicia has. I don't work outside of the home, therefore I don't have my own income, therefore I do not have my own financial freedom. Whereas, Alicia works outside of the home, she earns a paycheck, and she has established herself so that she can maintain financial freedom. So maybe I have security, but Alicia has the freedom . . . because my husband holds the purse strings. I admire my sister in that she has managed to make her own way and establish herself to the point where she has her own financial power and freedom—where I don't know that I know how to do that.

Both sisters are aware that they have different strengths and divergent lifestyles, but these differences neither jeopardize nor interfere with their close connection. They may still lapse into comparisons, as twins often do, but their affection for each other is unwavering. Alicia told me, "I have to say, my sister and I really don't have any problems; we just get along. As different as our lives are, we just see eye to eye. At this point in our lives, I think we both are happy with where we are." The years of comparing her situation unfavorably to Cheryl's gave way to a fulfilling new career for Alicia and a sense of herself as an accomplished individual. She also takes pride in the fact that her colleagues know her as an individual and value her for her singular personality. Cheryl not only admires her sister's financial autonomy and professional expertise, she is also inspired by Alicia's determination and success. Rather than feeling jealous of Alicia's financially independent status, Cheryl sees her as a role model. She respects her as an individual and treasures her as a sister. "To be honest," she said, "I just think it has been the greatest blessing to be a twin."

Alicia's need to earn more money for her family opened the door to self-discovery. She learned that she could further her education, begin a new career in her midthirties, and excel at something she finds fulfilling.

She values the work she does not simply because of the paycheck but because she has carved out a path that reflects her unique aspirations and skills. Rather than perceiving herself as the twin who could never quite measure up to her sister's lifestyle, she now takes pride in her hard-won individuality.

Various Paths to Claiming Your Self

Claiming your self and being independent from your twin is not a function of physically separating from or spending less time with her or him. Alicia and Cheryl live near each other and spend much of their free time with each other's families, but because their sense of who they are as individuals has evolved over the years, each has developed an inner separateness. Twins may live next door to one another or work together every day and still maintain that inner separateness, that sense of self that allows you to know who you are as an individual. Granted, it might be more of a challenge if your lives are tied closely together. But claiming your self isn't about moving away from your twin; it is an internal process that involves honestly confronting questions such as, how do I define myself as a person? How do I feel about my relationship to my twin? Does our twinship hold me back? Does it prevent me from being who I want to be?

In the preceding chapters, we've witnessed how various twins have claimed their individuality despite having faced particular twin-related issues. Sometimes emotional separation from one's twin is instigated by a physical move; in other instances, self-reflection, therapy, or a deliberate shift in personal aims can lead to a stronger sense of self.

In chapter 7, we heard about Miranda and Chloe, who recognized that their relationship has the potential to become overly close and overwhelming to their husbands, so they work to keep it in balance. Living in the same duplex was untenable—but so was living on opposite coasts. The sisters are incredibly close and acknowledge that they could not be happy living that far from one another; but in order for each to preserve her sense of self, they need the space to live separate lives. They are aware of the personal boundaries each requires, and both know what they must do to maintain a balance between connection and separation.

In chapter 4, Gail was devastated when her twin sister, Fran, moved away. The sisters had been in business together and Gail feared she couldn't make a go of it, personally or professionally, without her twin. She soon realized, however, that Fran's absence allowed her to develop her own unique talents and strengths. Gail is now proud of the fact that customers flock to her boutique thanks to her innovations, not because they are attracted to "the twins' store." She still misses Fran but appreciates that they live within a day's drive so they can see each other as often as they like.

Peter and Richard's story in chapter 5 pointed to the need for one twin to let go of guilty feelings about being more successful than his same-age sibling. Richard came to realize that he could not truly claim his sense of self until he relinquished his feelings of responsibility for how different his brother's life had turned out. Although Richard's guilty feelings stemmed from his love and empathy for Peter, he had to let go of the guilt that served only as an unhealthy connection to his brother. Richard learned that he was entitled to owning his success without feeling bad about it and that his brother was capable of making his way on his own terms.

Katherine explained in chapter 2 that part of the reason she and her twin sister, Hayley, were able to maintain their sense of individuality was that as teenagers they made a pact to treat each other as friends, not family. Due to their family history, the sisters believed that too often relatives feel entitled to be judgmental and critical, whereas friends are more likely to be respectful and supportive of each other. Throughout their lives, Hayley and Katherine have related to one another with an attitude of love and support, which has enabled each sister to grow as an individual.

In chapter 6, Ray acknowledged that he craved the closeness of a twin-like romantic relationship. But he has also developed his sense of self to the extent that he is committed to finding a significant other with whom he can enjoy a balance between closeness and individuality.

Nancy's physical split from her twin sister, Tamara, at the age of twenty-eight involved a heated dispute with her parents, even though both sisters were in favor of finally living apart. In chapter 4 we heard how a visit to a twins' festival, where twins of all ages dressed alike and reveled in their twinness, served as a catalyst for the sisters' decision. Later, after Tamara married and had children, Nancy defended her right to an independent life by refusing to move to the suburbs and become her niece and nephew's weekend baby-sitter. In so doing, Nancy further developed a sense of her own autonomy.

"He's Who He Is and I'm Who I Am"—Drew and Dennis

Fierce political arguments can tear apart family relationships—unless relatives understand that you don't have to be on the same page politically in order to respect and care about each other. It can be particularly challenging for twins to reach that understanding, but Drew and Dennis, fifty-year-old twin brothers, have successfully met that challenge. Drew is a proud liberal, Dennis a staunch conservative. They couldn't disagree more, yet their friendship is, to use Drew's word, "unassailable." Drew told me about a recent incident involving some rather pointed political name-calling:

> In the context of one of our heated debates, my brother said to me, "You probably think you're part of the liberal elite, don't you?" and without hesitation, I said, "Yes, I do." He meant it as an indictment, but for me I do feel enlightened, and I am educated, and I do have a progressive perspective on the world—so it was a compliment to me, even though it was used in a pejorative way.

Some might have taken Dennis' "pejorative" comment as an affront, but Drew wasn't offended in the least. Not only did he consider the remark a compliment, as mentioned above, but he and his brother are so secure in their individual identities and so close as brothers that even major political differences are "no big deal." When I interviewed Dennis separately, he referred to Drew as "a big lefty do-gooder" with whom he has had "some knock-down, drag-out conversations about politics." Drew told me he and his brother represent "the red and the blue" that color the political map of the United States. They fight over political issues and neither gives an inch, both accepting the indisputable fact that they are very different when it comes to their worldview.

I asked Drew how he and his brother are able to maintain their close connection given such disparate perspectives. They are used to having battles of one sort or another, he explained, but the differences that define who they are as individuals never seem to interfere with their friendship.

> It's like when we were younger. We used to just beat on each other, and then we'd skulk away, or my mom would separate us, and then five minutes later we'd go, "You wanna go play catch?" So, it just sort of washes off. It doesn't damage the relationship; it doesn't impact anything. Our arguments are sort of separate and apart. So even though we hold very different and strongly held opinions, it doesn't seem to be a big deal. Our friendship is unassailable.

When I talked to Dennis, he mentioned the brothers' different academic aptitudes, which became apparent in college, and how those may have impacted their divergent philosophical slants. He also referred to how the brothers had found their own peer groups in college:

> Drew was more the right side of the brain, the creative side, and I was definitely the other. He was more the creative, I was more the financial. During college, we were on the same campus, but the campus was so humongous that even though we were in the same fraternity and had many of the same friends, we also developed our own circle of friends.

They may each have had their own circle of friends in high school and college, but they were always each other's closest friend—and still are. As independent as each brother has become, and as different as they are from each other in many ways, they appreciate how they are able to "lean on" one another and be understood by the other. Dennis spoke of how deeply he values their empathic connection:

> I know for me, if I'm having a great day or if I'm having a terrible day, there's two calls to be made: one to my wife and one to my brother, and that's who I share it with. If I were a singleton, I might be searching for a best friend, but I've already got one—a built-in one . . . Sometimes he's calling me to lean on me and sometimes I'm calling him to lean on him. Somehow my brother and I have both had a lot of that, and there's so much empathy around the good or the bad, whatever's going on in the other person's life. And I think it's genuine, heartfelt.

Dennis and Drew's intimate friendship extends to the closeness each feels toward the other's children, something some singletons may have difficulty understanding. Dennis explained using the following example:

> Drew recently sent me an e-mail telling me about his daughter being invited to the U.S. Olympic camp, and I was really excited. When my wife saw the e-mail, she said, "So is Drew kind of bragging a little bit to you?" and I'm like, "Are you kidding? I'm as joyous as he is about his daughter getting this." My wife saw it as something competitive, in a negative way, but I didn't at all. He and I have both reveled in the other's successes, including the successes of our nieces and nephews, and we're both that kind of special uncle, if you will. I guess that could happen with any siblings, not just twins, but it's happened with us, and it's fabulous.

The reason Dennis and Drew can be best friends without sacrificing their individuality is that they accept and respect their differences, without making a big deal out of it. In fact, they both joke about their polar-opposite positions on the "red versus blue" political spectrum. As children they headed in separate directions when they felt like it and came together when they wanted to. They practiced sports together at home and played different sports at school. Today, as then, they don't feel obligated or forced to take care of each other emotionally, but they do feel comfortable "leaning on" each other in bad times and "reveling" in each other's successes. Because each brother has a healthy sense of self, neither one lets their dissimilarities jeopardize their "unassailable," cherished friendship.

Healthy Twinships Are Not Identical

Earlier in the book, I explained how the twin mystique creates unrealistic expectations regarding how twins should relate to each other. We talked about how your parents, friends, and society at large may expect the two of you to be intimate soul mates forever, to be lost without the other, to know each other better than you know yourself. Perhaps you believe that a uniquely spiritual connection between you and your twin does, in fact, exist, and that nontwins could never experience it. My objective in writing this book was not to dispel that belief, although I don't happen to adhere to it myself. My aim was to help adult twins feel entitled to their individuality and to encourage them to discover it, regardless of how close they are with their twin. Throughout the book, we have focused on core issues that often stand in the way of adult twins claiming that individuality: the inability to be honest with your twin about problems in your twinship; enmeshment and codependency; feeling responsible for your twin's emotional or physical well-being; feeling compelled to compare yourself to your twin; seeking a twin-like friend or lover; and being unable to resolve conflicting loyalties. I hope that in the course of this book you have gained insight into how these issues can be confronted so your path toward discovering and claiming your self will be clear.

What I have come to realize in researching this book is that twins deal with the challenges of twinness in a variety of ways, depending on their particular personalities, family background, and life circumstances. Healthy twinships are as unique as the individuals who comprise them. Some twins would be miserable living across the country from each other; others are satisfied if they can connect across the miles online. For some twins, a daily phone call is a prized ritual; for others, once a week is plenty. Some twins have little in common and yet seek out each other whenever they need a shoulder to cry on or a buddy to celebrate with. Others feel they are on the same page about most matters while at the same time understanding that their twin's attitudes and feelings will never be a carbon copy of their own. Some same-age siblings claim never to have had a rough patch or serious conflict; others had to work through many of the issues highlighted in previous chapters. There are twins who are best friends and twins who are not; twins who travel together and twins who wouldn't dream of it; twins who consider themselves second parents to their nephews and nieces and twins who prefer night-clubbing to baby-sitting their brother or sister's children. What makes such disparate twinships healthy is that both siblings know who they are as individuals and can enjoy the relationship with their twin without feeling guilty, obligated, or intruded upon. Having a healthy relationship with your twin is about loving him or her, not needing that person to complete you.

A healthy relationship with your twin is also about exploring what your twinship means to each of you, without demanding that it necessarily mean the same thing. When you know yourself well enough to identify what you need and can communicate your needs to your twin without feeling you're going to destroy the twinship, you will open yourself to a more authentic relationship. When same-age siblings can really listen to—and hear—their twin's perspective, even if it diverges from their own, positive change is possible. The hope is that your connection will be based on honest feelings and shared history rather than on artificial expectations and obligation.

Self-Reflection and Twin Communication

When you understand the twin-related issues we've explored in this book, you will be much better equipped to handle them. Self-reflection is key to that understanding, and so is talking to your brother or sister about your feelings. Self-reflection is a tool every twin can use to explore troubling twinship issues, abandon self-reproach and blame, and move on to a more satisfying, genuine relationship with oneself and one's twin. Although it may seem that self-reflection is a simple, straightforward process, it can be difficult for a twin. If you have always experienced life as half of a unit ("the twins") rather than as an individual, and if you and your twin have been responsible for satisfying each other's primary emotional needs, reflecting on how your twinship has influenced who you are can be painful. Focusing on your personal history with your twin, acknowledging such issues as codependency, separation anxiety, caretaking, competition, and conflicting loyalties—and assessing the degree to which these problems are still unresolved—can be disturbing. However, the more self-reflective you are and the more honest you can be about your experience being a twin, the more easily you will be able to deal with the twin-related issues that may be holding you back from healthy relationships and a fulfilling life. Getting in touch with your feelings may not be easy, but ultimately it will allow you to gain more control over your life. On the other hand, if you don't confront the unresolved issues between you and your twin, and if you don't fully know yourself as an individual, you may unwittingly carry your twinship issues along with you as baggage throughout your life. You may not only act out those issues with other friends or partners, but your relationship with your twin will remain stuck.

Once you become clear about the problem areas in your twinship, you may be ready to sit down and talk to your brother or sister about your feelings and their feelings. The point isn't to get into an argument or refute your twin's perception of your twinship; rather, it is to express yourself honestly and listen openly to what your twin has to say. Understand that your brother or sister has his or her distinct perspective. The two of you may feel very differently about whether or not competition exists between you, about what each of you expects from the other, and about holding onto unwanted guilt or resentment. If you can accept that the two of you will disagree, and that you may draw differing portraits of the same relationship, you can prevent your conversation from becoming a quarrel.

When you each listen with an open mind and heart, you won't have to get defensive, and the conversation won't head off into "I'm right and you're wrong" territory. Try to accept that you and your twin each experience your twinship uniquely and that this is perfectly normal. In any relationship, two people rarely have the same perspective on how they relate to each other. When you are mindful of that, and if you approach the conversation with a nondefensive attitude, you will create the space to hear what your twin's thoughts and feelings are and be able to proceed from a place of acceptance and respect. Hearing each other's perspective without concluding that one person is wrong and the other is right opens the door to authentic understanding and a healthier twinship. Although this book focuses on twin-related problems encountered by adult twins, nearly every person with whom I spoke or who answered the survey referred to how much they appreciate being a twin, despite the challenges. They recognize that a twinship is a unique relationship, similar to a close, nontwin sibling relationship but special in many ways. Here are some excerpts from our Adult Twin Survey that testify to the exceptional qualities found in so many twinships:

- We've always had that sense that "As mad as I am right now, just give me some space—you know I love you and I'll always be there."

- Even though our judgments can be very harsh on each other, our mutual support is unswerving. There is the feeling of always having a warm presence in my life.

- We're best friends yet we have our own identities and lives. I feel blessed to have been born with my best friend.

- I love the fact that I was born a twin. My brother and I love to laugh and do so often at or with each other—we are our own best audience.

Our close relationship doesn't hold either of us back from our separate lives.

- I enjoy being a twin but sometimes I forget that we are. We are close but don't depend on each other. She lives in a different state and I enjoy traveling to see her. I think of her more as my best friend than a sister.

- I feel like she is the one person I can count on unconditionally as long as we both live.

- She is my best friend and I love her dearly. I think the distance has given us both the chance to grow as individuals.

- The bond I share with my twin brother is unbreakable. We have our own lives but we also share a very open relationship and are honest with our feelings. I couldn't have been more blessed being born as a twin. On cloudy days I have someone to talk to.

- I think about my twin every day, and even tiny, stupid things we say to each other, that are part of our twins' vocabulary, make me laugh!

- My twin and I have worked hard to make our relationship work in a healthy way and we're very much best friends. I would not be the strong woman I am today without her presence in my life all along.

- Me and my sister have disagreements on a regular basis but I couldn't imagine what life would be like without her. She will always be my best friend, no matter how mad I am at her.

- We have both struggled with depression and when one of us was a mess, it was almost impossible for the other of us not to struggle with our worry about the other. But as we've matured and grown, I've realized just how valuable and rare our relationship is and wouldn't trade it for the world.

- Being a twin has taken me to the extremes of feelings, from entirely frustrated to immensely rewarded and from lonely and lost in my identity to the security in always having a built-in friend.

- I love being a twin! My sister and I have learned how to grow separately and still remain in a close friendship.

And perhaps my favorite quote of all is this one: "When I'm driving in to work every day and I get that call from my sister—it's like taking a vitamin! I just love hearing her voice."

Each of these adult twins is expressing love for a person with whom they have shared milestones and challenges, laughter and quarrels, pain and delight throughout their lives. Their statements attest to the fact that although twinships may entail unique difficulties, when those problems are acknowledged and addressed, the way is cleared to enjoy a very special connection. A healthy twinship does not hold either sibling back from claiming one's self. Rather, a good relationship between adult twins enhances the individual lives of both people—through a sense of closeness and intimacy, an invigorating brotherly or sisterly love—like a twinship-infused vitamin.

Continuing the Process of Self-Discovery

Regardless of the particular external circumstance or internal epiphany that motivates you to discover and claim who you are as an individual, the discovery will be life-changing. Reading this book has likely been your first step. Here are some additional steps you can take to continue the process:

- Create opportunities to be known as an individual by getting involved on your own in sports, hobbies, classes, and travel.

- Nurture other meaningful relationships so you can experience closeness in a nontwin context.

- Be cognizant of your twin's needs for emotional and physical space when he/she is involved in other intimate relationships.

- Handle expectable feelings of resentment, disappointment, or disapproval with a professional or a confidant who that understands the challenges inherent in twin relationships.

Notes

1. Nicholas Bakalar, "Twin Births in the U.S., Like Never Before," *New York Times*, January 24, 2012.

2. Monica Hesse, "Digital Mashup for Facebook Duo; Unrelated Actors Play Twins in 'Social Network,'" *Washington Post*, October 1, 2010.

3. Jesse Ellison, "'Tyler Winklevoss, Zuckerberg's Nemesis," *Newsweek*, December 27, 2010, 55.

4. "Fred and George Weasley," The Harry Potter Lexicon, last updated July 8, 2012, http://www.hp-lexicon.org/wizards/twins.html.

5. "Jane," Twilight Wiki, last modified June 16, 2013, http://www.twilightsaga.wikia.com/wiki/Jane; and "Alec," Twilight Wiki, last modified June 11, 2013, http://www.twilightsaga.wikia.com/wiki/Alec.

6. "Patterns and Characteristics of Codependence," Co-Dependents Anonymous, accessed November 12, 2010, http://www.coda.org/tools4recovery/patterns-new.htm.

7. Sandbank, Audrey C., ed., *Twin and Triplet Psychology: A Professional Guide to Working with Multiples* (London: Routledge, 1999), 177.

8. "Enmeshment," MentalHelp.net, accessed October 15, 2010, www.mentalhelp.net/poc/view_index.php?idx=37&id=156.

9. Sandbank, *Twin and Triplet Psychology*, 183.

Index

About the Author

Dr. Joan A. Friedman is a gifted psychotherapist who has devoted many years of her professional career to educating twins and their families about twins' emotional needs. Having worked through her own twinship challenges and parented her fraternal twin sons, she is a definitive expert about twin development. She is the author of *Emotionally Healthy Twins: A New Philosophy for Parenting Two Unique Children*. She has spoken to culturally diverse groups of twins around the world. Dr. Friedman's current work focuses on issues that adult twins confront as they adjust to life as singletons after having been raised as twins.

Dr. Friedman would love to hear from other adult twins. You can reach her via Facebook (www.facebook.com/joanafriedmanphd), Goodreads (www.goodreads.com/user/show/21469578-joan-friedman), LinkedIn (www.linkedin.com/profile/view?id=45705813&trk=nav_responsive_tab_profile), Twitter (twitter.com/Joanafriedman), or her website (www.joanafriedmanphd.com).